Praise for
Get the Job You Want, Even Wh...

"*Get the Job You Want, Even When No One's Hiring* offers solid advice to help job seekers adjust their mind-sets while improving their skill sets. Beyond offering a comprehensive set of exercises, this book provides the tools to get you on track and keep you moving forward during these challenging times. Ford Myers' street smart techniques will help you take control of your career and succeed in your job search!"
—**Cheryl Bonner**, Director, Penn State Alumni Career Services

"*Get the Job You Want, Even When No One's Hiring* does two critical things as you navigate the toughest employment landscape in recent history: It sets real-world expectations and presents real-world solutions. Ford Myers' book does both of these things at a level of thoroughness that readers will really appreciate!"
—**Dave Opton**, Founder and CEO, ExecuNet

"*Get the Job You Want, Even When No One's Hiring* is a timely and important book that teaches you how to take charge of your career in hard times. Ford Myers is a master at transforming complexity into action and results. This down-to-earth, practical book lays out your path to career success for the rest of your professional life. I highly recommend it!"
—**Richard J. Leider**, Founder, The Inventure Group
and author of *The Power of Purpose and Repacking Your Bags*

"*Get the Job You Want, Even When No One's Hiring* is the ultimate guide for helping job seekers find better jobs in these extraordinarily difficult times. It's packed with practical, easy-to-understand instructions that walk the reader through the entire job search process. Equipped with these insights, you will be able to beat out your competition, land a better job, and earn more than you thought possible—even when it appears that no one's hiring!"
—**Michael T. Robinson**, Owner and Creator, CareerPlanner.com

GET THE JOB YOU WANT, EVEN WHEN NO ONE'S HIRING

GET THE JOB YOU WANT, EVEN WHEN NO ONE'S HIRING

Take Charge of Your Career, Find a Job You Love, and Earn What You Deserve!

FORD R. MYERS

John Wiley & Sons, Inc.

Published by John Wiley & Sons, Inc., Hoboken, New Jersey.
Published simultaneously in Canada.

For general information on our other products and services or for technical support, please contact our Customer Care Department within the United States at (800) 762-2974, outside the United States at (317) 572-3993 or fax (317) 572-4002.

Wiley also publishes its books in a variety of electronic formats. Some content that appears in print may not be available in electronic books. For more information about Wiley products, visit our web site at www.wiley.com.

Library of Congress Cataloging-in-Publication Data:

Myers, Ford R., 1954-
Get the job you want, even when no one's hiring : take charge of your career, find a job you love, and earn what you deserve! / Ford R. Myers.
p. cm.
Includes index.
ISBN 978-0-470-45741-2 (pbk.)
1. Job hunting. I. Title.
HF5382.7.M94 2009
650.14–dc22

2008054900

Printed in the United States of America.

10 9 8 7 6 5 4

This book is dedicated to my parents, whose constant support has seen me well through the journey.

CONTENTS

ACKNOWLEDGMENTS

I would like to express my appreciation to the people who helped in the development and publication of *Get the Job You Want, Even When No One's Hiring*.

To David Newman, Consultant and friend, for contributing so much to the book's content and structure—and for helping to bring the original vision into reality.

To Bob Silverstein, Literary Agent at Quicksilver Books, for his steadfast belief, loyal support and wise counsel.

To Richard Narramore, Senior Editor at John Wiley & Sons, for seeing the merit of this project and providing keen editorial insight.

To Ann Kenny, Editorial Assistant, and Kate Lindsay, Production Editor, both at John Wiley & Sons Inc., for facilitating the process and keeping things moving along.

To my clients, whose honesty, courage, commitment and hard work continue to inspire me.

ABOUT YOUR JOB SEARCH SURVIVAL TOOLKIT

On page 32, you'll see the first reference to this web link: **www.CareerPotential.com/bookbonus**. This link appears many times throughout the rest of the book. Visiting this web page gives you instant access to your "Job Search Survival Toolkit," which includes a whole array of downloadable examples, exercises, and forms. These interactive resources will make it much easier for you to develop your own "Toolkit," and they'll also save you an enormous amount of time and effort. Be sure to take full advantage of these value-added, online elements of the book, all of which are designed to help you get the job you want, even when no one's hiring.

GET THE JOB YOU WANT, EVEN WHEN NO ONE'S HIRING

PART I

The Psychology of Job Hunting in a Down Market

1. Yes, The Job Market Is Bad—*Really* Bad!

As of this writing, the United States is experiencing its worst economy since the Great Depression. The stock market just had the largest one-day drop in history and fluctuates wildly based on the daily economic news, which seems to get increasingly worse. Investors have already lost more than 7 trillion dollars, and the shockwaves of the credit crunch are reverberating across the country and around the globe.

Governments are being forced to bail out entire industries and invest directly into financial institutions to keep them afloat. Our very notions of government agencies and private businesses are in the process of being redefined.

Millions of U.S. citizens can't pay their mortgages or are actually losing their homes with an unprecedented number of foreclosures and bankruptcies. Parents can't pay their children's tuition bills. Entire retirement funds are being decimated on Wall Street.

The job market is weaker than it has been in 80 years. The U.S. recession has claimed more than 4 million jobs to date. More than 4 million jobs have been lost in a one-year period. One hundred forty-five thousand positions were recently eliminated in ***just one week***, with nearly 650,000 jobs lost *within one month*. Unemployment continues to expand with more layoffs and downsizings. As the economy shrinks, debt soars, and the headlines proclaim one financial meltdown after another. Worst of all, it seems that *no one's hiring!*

Perhaps most startling of all, the United Nation's International Labor Organization estimates that the current financial crisis will add at least 20 million people to the world's unemployed, bringing the total to 210 million by the end of 2009.

So let me be clear: if you're feeling that something is very, very wrong with your quest to take charge of your career, find a job you love, and earn what you deserve, you're right. But it's not your fault. We are in the middle of a perfect storm, and it's almost surely going to get worse before it gets better.

2. It's Okay to Feel Frustrated, Depressed, Afraid, Helpless, or Disoriented

No one knows what's going to happen next. For working people everywhere, these are very challenging times indeed. Everyone is concerned, even those who still have jobs. Some folks are terrified, especially those who have been out of work for a while.

> If you're feeling frustrated, depressed, afraid, helpless, or disoriented, you're certainly not alone.

These reactions are understandable and to be expected. If you're feeling frustrated, depressed, afraid, helpless, or disoriented, you're certainly not alone. You might even feel angry or victimized. Perhaps you're saying things to yourself such as, "This shouldn't be happening to me! I got a good education. I worked hard. I always did the right thing, and I don't deserve this. I never thought I'd be in this situation. Maybe this is what happens to *other* people, but not *me*!"

Sound familiar? This is what I've been hearing from many of my career coaching clients in recent months. It's like a nightmare that we're all hoping to awaken from. Quite candidly, several clients have spent their recent career coaching sessions crying, and my office has been going through a box of tissues every few days. Believe me, *I get it!*

My clients need comfort and reassurance. My guess is that you do, too. So, let me tell you the same things I've been telling my clients. It's okay to have all of the reactions listed earlier and any other emotions you might be experiencing. There's nothing wrong with you, and you didn't do anything to bring this fate upon yourself. You're still a good person, and you still have all of the qualities, experiences, and credentials you had before. Although it may be difficult to believe right now, this awful employment situation will come to an end, and your career *will* get back on track—eventually.

This awful employment situation will come to an end, and your career *will* get back on track.

3. This Has Happened Before, and It Will Happen Again

How do I know you'll get back on track? Because I've been working as a career coach for many years, and my practice has gone through several economic downturns. Through it all, I've helped thousands of people take charge of their careers, find jobs they love, and earn what they deserve. So here's a question for you: Given how difficult things are now, how do *you* want to react, and what do you want to do to improve *your* career situation?

I firmly believe that you have a choice and that the choice you make will determine the outcomes of your job search. Some people will panic and sit on the sidelines, waiting for the situation to change. Others will remain in a state of denial, acting as though world events can't affect them. Still others will assess the employment situation for what it is, and then do whatever it takes to rise above their circumstances and create success.

What's needed is *action*, and you don't have to take on the challenge alone. All of the help, support, tools, and resources you need are available to you. It's up to you to find and take advantage of them. This book offers you a lifeline. If you're willing to adopt a new attitude, shift your assumptions, step a bit outside of your comfort zone, try a few new behaviors, and use some new tools—you *will* get the job you want, even when no one's hiring.

4. Why Your Chances Are Better Than You Think

It may have been more accurate to entitle this book "Get the Job You Want, Even When *You Think* No One's Hiring." That's because it's a false assumption to say that "no one's hiring," regardless of how bad the economy and job market may seem. The fact is that every company is hiring all the time, if you can offer precisely what they need when they need it.

> The fact is that every company is hiring all the time, if you can offer precisely what they need when they need it.

I'm not talking about job openings that are posted on company web sites or on Internet job boards. I'm not even talking about positions that are represented by executive recruiters. When it seems that no one's hiring, it is important *not* to focus just on job openings. There will be few publicly posted opportunities, and the competition for those few openings will be fierce.

Instead, you should work on identifying the particular needs, problems, and challenges that companies face during a serious market downturn. If you can demonstrate to the employer how you would address their issues successfully—and in the process make their company more productive, efficient, or profitable—you'll be able to land a good job in *any* economy. Of course, this approach requires that you take full responsibility for your own career, and that you learn to sell your value in a compelling way. But this approach can also liberate you from the fear of facing unemployment every time the job market shrinks.

So, keep a close watch on your own assumptions. Study this book, and implement all of the strategies I've outlined for you. While others are sitting on the sidelines, convinced that there are no good jobs to be had, you'll be out there getting the job you want. Rather than feeling helpless, you'll regain your sense of empowerment and control. *What a relief!*

5. The Number-One Secret to Job Search Success

What you are about to read, study, and work on *should be* taught in schools. But it's not. We go through 12 years of education, possibly four more years of college, and sometimes even two to four *more* years of graduate school, and not one day is spent on how to manage your career, find work you truly enjoy, and make sure you're well compensated for it. Not *one* day!

Employers should teach this material, too. It's to every employer's advantage to make sure that their people are proactively managing their careers, are doing work they're well-suited for, and are equipped to perform at their full potential. But, of course, *they* don't teach these secrets and strategies either. Not even *one day* is spent teaching employees these vital skills!

Once you understand and start to use these secrets, you'll have a powerful advantage at every point in your career. This is *not* just a book to help you get your next job (although it will certainly do that). It's a resource to help you *always* get the *right* job and manage your career in a much more effective way—even in the toughest job market, even during a financial meltdown, and even when no one's hiring.

> This insider's handbook shows you all of the things that are absolutely necessary to know and that should have been taught in school or by your employer—but weren't.

You might be asking, "Where did all of this material come from, and why should I buy into it?" After working at three of the nation's largest career consulting companies for almost 15 years, I saw the need for a new approach—an approach that would combine the methods and resources of large outplacement firms with the personal attention and flexibility of small career counseling practices. This new concept became my proprietary, five-phase career success process called *Career Potential*SM—a process that consistently produces outstanding job search results.

Would you like to know the number-one secret of how to get a job when no one's hiring? Would you like to know the key—and sometimes the *only*—difference between people who are out of work for three months and three years? It's simple: **Mind-set comes before skill set**.

Want proof? In addition to the hundreds of frontline folks and mid-level managers I've worked with, I've also worked with dozens of very senior executives who earn high six-figure salaries. Regardless of the economy, regardless of the unemployment statistics from the federal government, and regardless of how tough the media keeps saying the job market is, these high flyers are rarely out of work for more than a few months.

> Mind-set comes before skill set.

Is it because they are more qualified than most? No. Have better job skills? No. Savvier networking strategies? No. Is it because they're smarter? No. Better connected? No. More employable? No, it's not that either. The reason that many of my senior executive clients land jobs when no one's hiring is that they *expect* to get a job when no one's hiring. Their belief system is 100 percent wired to support their success: mindset comes before skill set.

The same thing applies to *you*! No matter where you are in your career and no matter what your salary level, if you have the right mindset, you'll *accelerate* your job search and *elevate* yourself over other candidates in all sorts of tangible and intangible ways. The book you're holding in your hands right now provides you with both the mindset *and* skill set to take charge of your career, find a job you love, and earn what you deserve. It was created to be the *only* book you'll need to get you through this employment crisis, and to help you navigate successfully through the rest of your career.

Starting right this moment, you have access to all of the same secrets, strategies, tips, and tools that I share with my executive clients who pay premium coaching fees for this privileged information. I'm confident that, by leveraging all of this material to the fullest extent, you'll produce the same kind of breakthrough career results that my clients do.

6. Tough Times Highlight the Difference Between Your Job and Your Career

For decades, people thought that doing their job—and doing it well—was sufficient to ensure long-term career success, plenty of financial reward, and job security well into the future. Here is what that picture looked like:

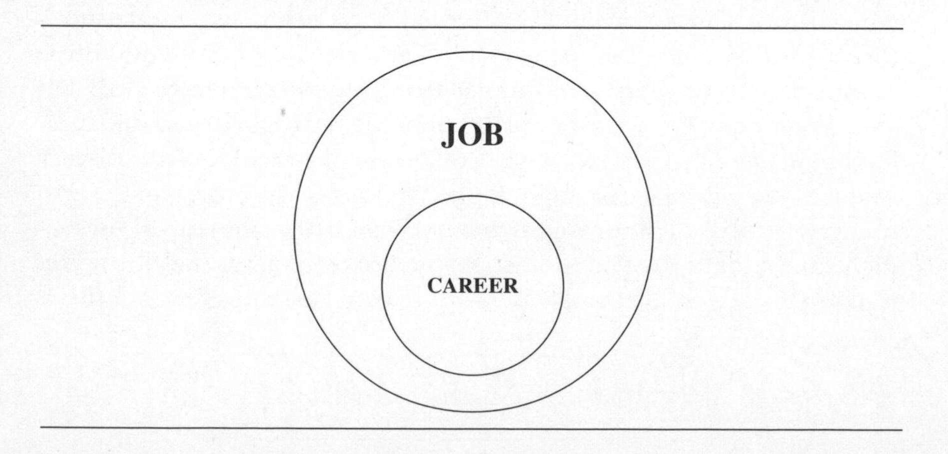

In this model, managing your career was only a tiny piece of the picture—something that rarely came into play. You would only think about career management when it came time to stop working for a time (in the case of parents wishing to stay home with children, for example) or under extremely unusual circumstances (such as when someone wanted to actually *change careers*!).

Today, working professionals may change careers five to seven times before retirement. You read that correctly—they change *careers*, not *jobs*, an average of five to seven times! Many people are still only equipping themselves to deal with the old paradigm and are unprepared to navigate in the new reality of career management, which looks more like this diagram:

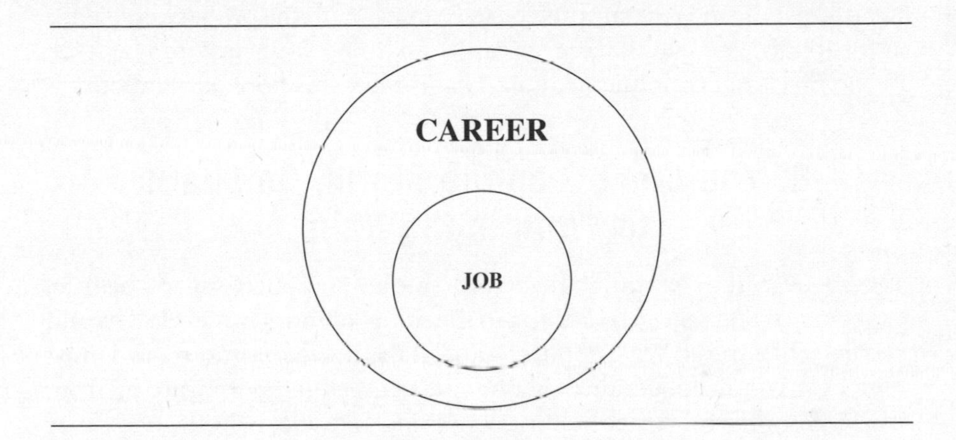

7. Most Job-Hunting Advice Doesn't Apply in a World Turned Upside Down

You get your clothes cleaned when they're dirty. You pay your bills each month. You see your doctor once or twice a year. You send cards to family members at each birthday. So, why is it that most people (maybe even you!) don't integrate "careering" (savvy career management activities) into their regular routines?

Most individuals have a reactive—not a proactive—approach to their careers. Thinking that you only need to fix your career when it's broken (i.e., when you're laid off, downsized, or just plain miserable) is a very unfortunate misconception that will seriously limit your career success—both now and in the future, when economic conditions start to improve.

> Thinking that you only need to fix your career when it's broken is a very unfortunate misconception.

Maybe you're in **career transition** (laid off, downsized, unemployed, between jobs, or changing industries); perhaps you're **underemployed** (not enough challenge, growth, or compensation in your current job); or you might be **fully employed**, but dissatisfied (wondering if there's something better for you elsewhere, or concerned that you made some wrong career choices).

Whichever situation you find yourself in, there are proven (and sometimes contrarian) steps you can take to maximize your opportunities and get the most from your chosen career. With the proper knowledge and support, you can make your career anything you want it to be, even in the midst of economic turmoil. That's what this book is all about.

8. You Can't Stop the Storm, So Learn to Work in the Rain

This book will help you change your thinking about your job search, especially when you're searching in the midst of market meltdowns and record joblessness. We'll debunk some of the most common—and most dangerous—misconceptions about career management, drawing from my 15 years of experience helping people just like you, in both good times and times of great economic disruption.

Even though this may be the most emotionally draining and financially challenging time of your life, we'll work together to get you back into a winning mindset with a concrete, positive plan to generate results as quickly as possible. Then we'll dig into step-by-step strategies to get you grounded, focused, and ready to embark on the systematic process of getting a job when no one's hiring.

9. How You Can Get a *Better* Job *Faster* When Times Are Tough

When times are tough and things look bleak, that's the time to push harder than ever. Let me show you why this is so. Are you depressed that you didn't ace your last job interview? Are you feeling like a failure because the job that looked so good went to another candidate?

> When times are tough and things look bleak, that's the time to push harder than ever.

It's tempting to just give up and feel sorry for yourself, isn't it? Well, a lot of people are doing exactly that—they're not pushing as hard and coasting, or wallowing in self-pity and bad TV reruns. They're exhausted, tapped out, and tired of the rejection they've been feeling in the job market.

When the job market is down and your competition has decided to sit out the rest of the game, that's the worst time for *you* to quit, because now you can have everyone's attention. There's actually much less noise out there for your message to compete against. Push now, and you'll be heard. Leverage smart career strategies, and you'll get noticed.

10. When No One's Hiring, Focus and Clarity Are More Important Than Ever

When the economy is in bad shape, when unemployment numbers start to climb, and when no one's hiring, many well-qualified, highly educated, and hardworking people start to lower their sights. Any job becomes preferable to no job in the name of paying the bills. Getting another position (*any* position) as quickly as possible appears to make sense, because of the old advice that you can always keep looking, and it's easier to get a new job when you currently have a job.

This is flawed thinking, and I've seen it backfire too many times not to warn you against it. If you take the first job that comes along, you'll get complacent. Inertia and fear will set in. I understand that in the short term, it will feel a lot easier to go to a job each morning than to work hard on taking charge of your career, finding a job you love, and earning what you deserve. But as weeks turn into months and months turn into years, you may find yourself stuck in that job you took for the sake of paying the bills. Pretty soon, you will have lost your career bearings, and with every passing day, the notion of changing lanes will become more unpleasant and scary.

> As weeks turn into months and months turn into years, you may find yourself stuck in that job you took for the sake of paying the bills.

11. Your Attitude and Assumptions Will Dictate Your Career Fate

When no one's hiring, you need to be *more* selective in your job search. You need to focus like a laser on exactly the kind of work you would *love* to do. You need to identify precisely the kind of company you want to hire as your next employer. And you need to be crystal clear on the ideal work situation for you. Your attitude, assumptions, and beliefs alone will determine how far you carry this material—and how quickly. As Henry Ford said, "Whether you think you can or you think you can't, you're right."

Your level of focus and clarity will come through in every phase of the job search that you'll read about in the coming chapters. Hiring managers will be able to sense your focus, clarity, and commitment. Unlike your competition in a job market where no one's hiring, *you* will exude confidence, focus, and fit because you've laser-targeted the precise kind of job where you can do your very best work and deliver maximum value to your employer and customers. Mindset before skill set. Throughout the rest of this book, keep one thought in mind: **You can do this!**

12. Seven Truths of Career Success, for Both Good Times and Bad

1. The Most Qualified Candidate Does Not Necessarily Get the Job Offer

Many times, candidates with lesser qualifications get job offers simply because they've prepared and presented themselves in a more compelling way. In other words, they're better self-marketers than the other candidates. In a tight job market, being qualified is never enough. You must *demonstrate* to the employer that you're the best candidate for the job. Depending on your age and how your parents raised you, you may be operating under a wishful thinking mindset regarding the concept of *meritocracy*. This would include the following cultural messages and ingrained assumptions that many of us were taught repeatedly over the years by well-meaning parents and teachers:

- Getting good grades guarantees success in college and in life.
- Being smart means that you'll do better than people who are not smart (or at least not *as* smart as you).

- Hard work is its own reward—and is also the best path to other rewards.
- Achievement and recognition go hand-in-hand. In other words, just do well, and other people (e.g., teachers, professors, employers, bosses, the CEO) will recognize and reward you for it.

In a difficult employment landscape, strong qualifications and accomplishments are *necessary, but not sufficient*, to find a job you love and earn what you deserve.

In a difficult employment landscape, strong qualifications and accomplishments are necessary, but not sufficient, to find a job you love and earn what you deserve.

Let's say that you're competing against another candidate whose qualifications are just as strong as yours. What is the hiring manager supposed to do? Well, the answer is obvious: he or she will be influenced by how good a job you do in marketing, selling, and positioning those strong qualifications. At the end of the day, the best self-marketer gets the job. We'll talk a lot more about self-marketing tools and strategies as we progress through the rest of this book.

But for now, don't be fooled into believing that the business world is a meritocracy, because it's not. That can be either good news or bad news, depending on how you've positioned yourself up to this point in your career. But don't worry, we'll boost your self-marketing skills to the point where you can land a great job regardless of the economic climate, unemployment news, or latest Wall Street implosion.

2. The Best Time to Work on Your Career Is When Your Job Is Secure

Even if you're very happily employed today, you never know what may happen tomorrow. To avoid a career disaster, you should incorporate the concept of Perpetual Career Management into your professional life. Vital tasks like keeping your success stories up to date, or networking regularly with professionals in your industry, should be incorporated into your routine whether the economy is good or bad—and whether you feel you need to or not.

Here's a real-life example: A few years ago, I had a client who was in a senior-level sales and marketing position at a large manufacturing company. He had everything going for him with the employer: he was a member of the senior management team, he had been with the firm for 13 years, and he was consistently praised for his hard work and professionalism. Needless to say, he felt very comfortable and secure in his position. He never saw what was about to happen.

Due to an economic downturn and an eventual acquisition of the company, my client was suddenly laid off on a crisp November morning. An hour later, he found himself sitting in his car in the parking lot, asking himself over and over, "How could this have happened? I did such a good job for them!" And worst of all, my client was totally unprepared! He had none of the tools necessary to find another appropriate position within a reasonable period of time. Naturally, he felt concerned and scared. He later told me that the toughest part of his situation was feeling completely helpless.

What does this mean for you? It means that you should consider adopting a different approach, the Perpetual Career Management approach—not only to avoid feeling helpless, but to truly take charge of your career once and for all. *Note*: We'll be talking a lot more about Perpetual Career Management in Part V of this book.

As we said earlier, instead of focusing completely on your job, you should focus on managing your career—at all times, regardless of where the economy or job market happens to be. That's the key that will help you to chop months off your next job search, significantly boost your salary, get promoted faster, and never worry again about job security or layoffs.

> Instead of focusing completely on your job, you should focus on managing your career—at all times, regardless of where the economy or job market happens to be.

3. Graduating from School Is the Beginning of Your Education, Not the End

In good economic times or bad, you should always look for ways to advance your industry knowledge and professional qualifications. Attending seminars, reading trade journals, pursuing certifications, and so on—these activities should be a part of your ongoing professional development process. It's imperative that every professional remain current in his or her field. No company wants to hire a candidate whose base of knowledge is out of date. Moreover, why would your *current* organization and *current* boss want to work with someone like that? *Not* upgrading your knowledge and skills continually is a risk you can't afford to take.

As a professional, you should continually build your credentials, which will make you more attractive and marketable as a candidate—both inside your company and in the outside world.

> *Not* upgrading your knowledge and skills continually is a risk you can't afford to take.

Plus, in a down economy, the greatest asset you have to sell is your knowledge and intellectual resources. When business gets tough, the demand for people who can think strategically and deliver results goes *up*, not down.

4. An Employer's First Offer Is *Never* Its Best Offer

Employers expect that you've done salary research, and they *anticipate* having dynamic negotiations with you. In fact, they'll often be *disappointed* and question your candidacy if you *don't* negotiate—even when no one's hiring. You might be tempted to think that any job offer is great in a tough economy or that this is the worst time to negotiate, but you would be dead wrong.

Employers usually start with a low salary offer merely as a trial balloon, to see how you'll react, and there's almost always room to improve on the initial compensation offer, even in a tight job market. In a way, compensation negotiation is a game, with its own set of rules and guidelines. We'll get into the detailed negotiation tactics you need later in this book, but for now, be aware that the first offer is merely a starting point. If you don't negotiate further, I guarantee that you'll be leaving money—and possibly a whole lot more—on the table.

5. Always Research and Be Plugged In to the Competition

Research and be aware of the competition—whether it be information about other companies or other professionals in your industry. Always know who they are and what they're doing. Endeavor to know the competition better than they know themselves. This will greatly enhance your competitiveness when jobs are hard to come by, and it will allow you to jump on opportunities that others might not yet be aware of.

> If you don't negotiate, I guarantee that you'll be leaving money—and possibly a whole lot more—on the table.

Here's an example of how important it is to be plugged into your competitors. One of my clients is the president of a small advertising agency. Her client base is solid, her creative work is excellent, and she makes a very good living in this role. But the thing that my client is most proud of is the fact that her firm is the envy of every small- to medium-sized agency in town—not because of the creative awards my client has won, and not because of how impressive her offices are, although these are certainly noteworthy achievements. My client is so envied because she always seems to get the most prestigious accounts and the most interesting assignments. My client also has a real knack for getting the best designers in the region to work for her. The other agency owners in the region just stand around, shaking their heads in disbelief and frustration. "How does she do it?" they ask themselves, repeatedly.

Well, just between you and me, it's not because my client's work is so much better than the work of the other agencies. No, the way she keeps winning, over and over, is that her investigative research is superior to that of any of her competitors. She makes it her business to know what's going on in her market—what company is doing what, which accounts are going where, who's working for whom, what challenges or trends are affecting local companies, and all the rest. The bottom line is simply that my client is far more plugged in, and she has used this knowledge to beat out the competition continually.

So what does this mean to you? It means you should start to research your way to success. Read industry publications, trade magazines, your local business journal, your daily newspaper's business section, *Business Week, Fortune, Forbes*, the *Wall Street Journal*, and so on. Pay attention to other local, regional, and national sources of business intelligence, such as web sites, newsletters, blogs, and radio or TV shows. Learn to frame your expertise, your ideas, and your value in terms that are relevant to the current business and economic landscape.

> Learn to frame your expertise, your ideas, and your value in terms that are relevant to the current business and economic landscape.

Connect with people, companies, and groups that you read about. If you can move and shake with the movers and shakers, so much the better. If you can't, you should at least know what they're thinking, what they're concerned about, and what opportunities they see ahead. The more you know about the competition, the easier it will be to get a job when no one's hiring.

6. Networking Is Not as Important as You Think It Is

It is *more* important! Put time aside every week for active networking to maintain established relationships and develop new ones—both inside and outside of the company where you work. You should always be positioned to leverage your professional and personal contacts when the need arises. So, adopt the discipline of blocking out time on your calendar specifically for networking activities—every week, every month, and every year, for the duration of your career.

I'll never forget a story I heard when I was facilitating a job search team several years ago. We had about 15 people in the conference room. After I conducted a brief presentation about professional networking, one of the participants asked if she could share a personal story.

She said that she had just been laid off from her employer of almost 25 years. She had started at the company as an entry-level customer support representative. On that same day, another individual started at the company in the same job. They discovered that they were just about the same age, and that their backgrounds were very similar, in terms of education, interests, family history, and so on. My client and this man worked well together for about two years, when he was suddenly transferred to another department, and at a higher level, within the company.

She didn't see him much after that, but she did occasionally hear about how well he was doing with the firm. Years passed, until eventually she was laid off and came to my office in need of career help. "By the way," she said, "that man who started at the company with me became, and is still, the president of that company!" At the time of her layoff, on the other hand, my client had held the same position for which she was hired nearly 25 years ago. When I asked her to tell the group why she thought she had remained at the same level, while her colleague had moved up to claim the presidency of their company, she said, without hesitation, "Oh, that's an easy one. He was always a master networker. Me? I was just doing my job."

This story proves, without any doubt, how important it is to keep networking in both good economic times and bad—and to continually update your success file so that you can promote yourself to greater levels of responsibility.

> Adopt the discipline of blocking out time on your calendar specifically for networking activities—every week, every month, and every year, for the duration of your career.

7. If *You're* Not Managing Your Career, *Nobody* Is!

When I speak to audiences about career management strategies, I show a slide that has the following quiz on it:

QUIZ: Who is responsible for managing your career?

- ☐ Human Resources
- ☐ My Manager
- ☐ Recruiter
- ☐ Executive Search Firm
- ☐ Career Consultant
- ☐ None of the above

At different times and under different circumstances, perhaps any combination of these would have been the correct answer. But in today's economy, the answer is clearly "None of the above."

It doesn't matter what your Human Resources department says about "succession planning" or "leadership development" or "career pathing." It doesn't matter that you have great relationships with recruiting firms, perhaps even the one that connected you with your current position (remember: recruiters work for employers, not for candidates). It doesn't matter if you're working with the world's best career coach. It doesn't even matter if your boss loves everything you're doing, has big plans for you, and has nothing but glowing praise for you at every performance review. The bottom line is that *you*, and *only you*, hold the keys to your career, your future, and your own brand of employment security, even if there is no longer such a thing as job security (and there isn't).

13. How Employers React When There Are More Workers Than Jobs

When there are many more workers than job openings, employers behave differently than they do in a healthy employment market. This is largely because the locus of control shifts from candidates to employers, and employers will have the sense that they can call the shots. These dynamics can pose serious challenges for job seekers.

> When there are many more workers than job openings, employers behave differently than they do in a healthy employment market.

Under these circumstances, here are some of the typical challenges job seekers will face at many companies:

- Employers will generally cut back on spending, contract in size, and squeeze efficiencies out of existing facilities and resources.
- Employers will cut salaries and benefits of whatever job openings they still have, with the belief that they will be able to attract quality candidates for a lot less investment.
- Employers will take longer to make hiring decisions, with the belief that they can afford to be picky.
- Employers will expect candidates to provide greater value by offering more experience, skills, and accomplishments.
- Employers will want candidates to produce stronger business results with less resources and staff, but to work at the same or even lower-level titles than they did before.
- Employers will tend to curtail promotions, raises, bonuses, and perks, taking the position that "our employees are lucky just to have jobs here."
- Employers will fill the few positions that do open up internally, because this is much less expensive than recruiting and hiring candidates from the outside.

- Employers will expect their staff to be more flexible and to make greater sacrifices to keep their jobs, including more relocations, heavier workloads, and greater travel demands.
- Employers will re-deploy talent by transferring employees from one division or department to another, where they can have the most impact.
- Employers will put greater emphasis on recruiting passive candidates (those who already have jobs) as opposed to considering unemployed candidates.
- Employers will reduce their investments in search firms and recruiting technologies, expecting that the best candidates will come to them.
- Employers will tend to focus exclusively on survival and shareholder value, and will stop paying attention to employee morale and staff retention.
- Employers will fill job openings only with candidates whose background and experience precisely match those required by the position.

14. Twenty Habits of Highly Effective Job Seekers in a Down Market

Even in a down market, job seekers and employees are *not* powerless or without recourse in dealing with the challenges listed so far. In fact, you have more control over your career circumstances than you might think. Following are some specific strategies and tactics that consistently generate strong results for job seekers when no one's hiring. *Note*: There are 38 additional tips in the Career Resources section toward the end of this book.

1. **Network, network, network.** Continually increase your level of networking and keep expanding your contact database. Reach out to reestablish and nourish business and personal relationships. Offer to help others, even if they're not in a position to help you (because what goes around comes around). There is no substitute for connecting with people one-on-one. Stay connected and don't isolate yourself. Being out of work does not mean you have to be

out of touch, so be sure to build and maintain your networking momentum.

2. **Seek help.** Get career support from a professional. A qualified career coach can better prepare you to land your next position. If career coaching is unaffordable for you, take advantage of the support provided by government programs, nonprofit agencies, job search groups, college/alumni career centers, or faith-based missions for the unemployed and underemployed. If you're thinking of changing industries, get some career testing. If you are struggling emotionally, get help from a mental health service provider.
3. **Read career books and attend career seminars.** Take advantage of learning opportunities to improve your job search and career management skills. Keeping informed of business trends will help you gain greater knowledge of the industries and careers that are poised for future growth. Stay plugged in to the market and your field to ensure that you'll be current and to maintain your intellectual capital. Apply what you learn to generate stronger search results.
4. **Leverage technology.** Utilize web sites and online services to connect with your industry and to build greater visibility. Create a career web site, using tools like VisualCV (www.visualcv.com) and LinkedIn (www.linkedin.com). Reach out through social networking sites, such as Facebook (www.facebook.com), MySpace (www.myspace.com), and Twitter (www.twitter.com). Keep in touch with colleagues consistently via e-mail. In addition to leveraging career portals and job boards, learn how to use online tools like blogs, wikis, and virtual job fairs. Focus on optimizing your online identity.
5. **Differentiate yourself.** Position yourself as an expert by writing articles, giving presentations, or teaching a class. Get involved in professional organizations, and assume leadership roles there. Do something noteworthy in your community that will garner special recognition and build your positive reputation. Focus on what makes you special, and build your brand within your industry.
6. **Use your time off wisely.** Pursue professional development by participating in classes, seminars, certifications, and industry conferences. Take advantage of free and low-cost programs to enhance your credentials. Explore more of your world to generate

new ideas. Do the important things that you never had time to do when you were working full-time. Enjoy the feeling of still being productive and making a contribution.

7. **Pursue a temporary, part-time, or contract position.** Volunteer, provide pro bono work, take on a consulting contract, or complete an internship or apprenticeship. This tactic is especially useful for those who wish to pursue a career in a different industry. Keep yourself in the game, so you won't lose traction in your career growth.
8. **Act with speed and urgency.** One way for you to get an edge over other candidates is to demonstrate that you're more serious and more determined than the competition. Show up earlier. Arrive more prepared. Move quickly and efficiently. Make an impression by being more responsive and assertive than the others.
9. **Take care of yourself.** Eat well, exercise, get plenty of rest. You'll need to be healthy and vital to maintain the pace of an active job search campaign. Stay in close touch with friends and family. Keep up with your interests, hobbies, and activities. Follow your normal routines, even as you work hard on getting the job you want. Maintain balance in your life, and don't let the job search become all-consuming.
10. **Be flexible and adaptable.** Consider shifting industries and/or being geographically mobile to open up more career possibilities, even if you would not ordinarily choose these options. Rather than waiting for the perfect opportunity, offer your skills to other industries and lend your experience to different positions. Do whatever you need to do (within reason) to keep your career intact and earn a living.
11. **Improve and enhance all of the documents in your career portfolio.** Now is the time to expand your career portfolio far beyond just the resume. You'll need a one-page professional biography, a collection of powerful accomplishment stories, a series of compelling cover letters, a page of professional references, a list of targeted employers, a 30-second commercial (elevator speech), and other items. Craft a unified package that consistently conveys a highly professional image of yourself.
12. **Identify industries that will emerge stronger when the market improves.** Research emerging opportunities and niches that will offer career growth, and position yourself to take advantage of these trends. (Healthcare, education, and security are some

fields that are expected to continue expanding.) If your field has collapsed, be sure to communicate your transferable strengths and the tangible value you offer, rather than focusing on the trade skills from your old industry. Adapt to the realities of the changing work world, rather than holding onto your old career identity out of fear, resentment, or even nostalgia.

13. **Practice interviewing and negotiation skills.** In an ideal world, you would have been practicing your interviewing and negotiation skills while you were fully employed, rather than waiting for a career crisis to arise. But now that the employment market is in crisis, it's that much more important to polish and perfect these skills. Solicit the help of a partner to role-play with you, and switch roles as needed with the questions and answers. Practice with an audio-recording device, and listen to yourself as you continually improve your performance.
14. **Be patient, but persistent.** When the job market is bad, employers will prolong the hiring process, and your search is bound to take longer than usual. There is not much a candidate can do to rush things, so you'll need to be patient. However, this does not mean you should sit by the phone waiting for the employer to contact you. You'll want to pursue two basic strategies: (1) Be persistent, but don't be a pest, as you follow up consistently on every opportunity; and (2) Don't put all your eggs in one basket. Instead, keep moving forward as you explore every appropriate opening you can find. One benefit of pursuing multiple positions is that if you don't get an offer, or if an employer never gets back to you, you won't feel crushed.
15. **Focus on tangible results and practical solutions.** In a healthy job market, candidates can market themselves with their employment history, education, and related assets. But when no one's hiring, there needs to be a relentless focus on tangible, positive results. The primary question in the employer's mind will be, "What can you do for me—now?" This means that you should zero in and quickly identify the employer's most pressing needs and challenges—and then explain exactly how your relevant accomplishments will allow you to successfully address those issues in the short term.
16. **Work from a budget.** Instead of going into a panic or worrying that you'll lose everything you've worked for, conduct a detailed analysis of your financial situation and develop a family budget.

You may discover that you're in a better financial position than you had thought. While you're in transition, cut back on expenses and live as frugally as you reasonably can. Examine and update this budget on a weekly basis. This sort of discipline will pay off by stretching your dollars and providing some peace of mind.

17. **Be kind to yourself.** Your experience of being out of work or looking for a new job will be determined by how you look at it. You have a choice. You can beat yourself up, feel like a loser, and be riddled with guilt and shame. Or, you can look at your situation in a more positive way. Realize that you are not to blame for the economic meltdown or the high unemployment numbers. You didn't do anything wrong, and you're still a highly qualified professional. There is no longer the same stigma there used to be about being unemployed, as almost every family in America will be touched by layoffs and downsizings. Forgive yourself, forgive your ex-employer, and forgive the world. Move on toward a better career future.
18. **Pay extra attention to your personal image.** First impressions count. Make a deliberate, consistent effort to present yourself in the best light. Ask yourself, "How can I enhance my attributes in the following areas: hair, eyeglasses, makeup, hands, clothes, shoes, accessories, posture, smile?" Now is the ideal time to take stock of your appearance, and make whatever changes you feel could improve your job search results.
19. **Watch your attitude.** Job search is really an inside game, especially when no one's hiring. That is, the outcome of your search will have much more to do with *how you think* about it than with the external circumstances of the job market. Avoid the gloom and doom messages disseminated by the media, and stay away from any negative people in your life who bring you down. Maintain a positive attitude, and never state anything negative or act desperate. Spend some time each day focusing in and recalibrating your internal attitude. Even if you're out of a job, you probably have many other wonderful things in your life, so remember to be grateful.
20. **Be philosophical.** Think of the old saying, "Things happen for a reason." It usually turns out to be true. Look at the big-picture view of your recent change in employment. If you're like a lot of my clients, after a time you may come to see this transition as

a blessing in disguise. Many candidates go on to find jobs that are better than the ones they had before. Others take the opportunity to explore new careers, rediscover their professional passions, and make important decisions. While you certainly didn't ask to be forced into a job search by the economic crisis, try to find the life lessons and new perspectives in this transition. Commit to yourself that, somehow, you will make this a rewarding and productive experience.

Conducting a successful job search campaign takes energy, discipline, and career support. Despite the pressures you may face in today's employment market, you must stay focused on your goals and *search smart*.

> By continuing to think strategically, and by consistently taking the initiative, you'll inevitably get the job you want.

15. Hidden Sources of Career Support, Information, and Advice

When you're looking for a new job, there are obvious places you'd normally go to for help and support, including career web sites, job fairs, the help wanted section of your newspaper, and possibly your friends and family. However, a wider array of resources is available to you than you may think. Some of the hidden sources of career information, support, and advice include the following:

- Government agencies (federal and municipal)
- Career coaches
- Nonprofit agencies
- Job search clubs and groups
- College/alumni career centers
- Faith-based missions for the unemployed and underemployed
- Library business departments
- Free and low-cost career seminars and professional development programs

- Online employment and business databases
- Business books, magazines, newsletters, and blogs
- Industry-specific networking functions
- Business conferences and expos

> When no one's hiring, you owe it to yourself to leverage all of these resources and leave no stone unturned.

PART II

From Desperation to Career Strategies for Tough Times

16. What Do You Really Want to be Doing When the Economy Turns Around?

In this section, we're going to deal with the reality of your situation on two different levels: (1) the short-term reality that you probably have a mortgage to pay, a family to feed, and bills that keep arriving in the mail; and (2) you really need to figure out what you want to be doing long term, and where you'd like your true professional path to take you. The danger, of course, is that if you don't know where you're going, then any path will do.

Working in this reactive mode is not a recipe for career success. But let's first deal with your short-term need to pay your bills. Until that's taken care of, the less urgent, yet more important tasks will never get done.

17. The Pay My Bills Strategy

When the job market is tight and the economy is in a downturn, it generally takes a longer period of time to find the job you want. This may be fine if you have enough money in the bank to draw upon during your transition. But if you can't live on savings until you land your real job, you'll probably want to do some sort of part-time or temporary work to tide you over. This strategy—sometimes called the bridge job—has become common over the past few years, and it can be very effective for people at all professional levels. This approach often includes a two-step path, starting with an interim role, and eventually leading to the ideal position.

I recently worked with a successful executive who had been Senior Vice President of an industrial manufacturing company. He had an excellent education, including a background as an engineer. When he lost his job, he took a part-time position at a local paint store. The money wasn't great, but it was enough to help pay his family's bills. Having this part-time job also gave my client a sense of pride, because he was doing what he could to provide for his family, and he was making a contribution in the business world. He also enjoyed meeting new people and even doing a bit of networking with customers. The job at the paint store gave my client the flexibility he needed to continue searching for the job he really wanted. The owner of the paint store tried on many occasions to promote him to full-time manager. The answer was always "No, thank you."

A key point for you to understand is that my client never confused the means with the ends. He kept his focus on finding the real job, and he eventually secured an excellent opportunity with more responsibility and higher compensation than he'd had at his last professional job. In this case, my client's positive attitude allowed him to reach his goal through a two-step plan. By taking a part-time, flexible job, he did what he needed to do to get the position he really wanted. My client didn't feel ashamed or embarrassed working in a position that could have been perceived as beneath him. He saw this strategy as a practical necessity, and it worked for him. In fact, when he reflects back on his temporary job at the paint store, he smiles and describes it as a great learning experience.

> If you're out of work now, what part-time or flexible work can you do to fill the gap until you land the job you want?

What about you? If you're out of work now, what part-time or flexible work can you do to fill the gap until you land the job you want? If you're fully employed but concerned about losing your job, what sort of opportunity could you pursue to earn additional income, should the need arise? Here are some interim strategies to find work and earn money:

- **Part-time or temporary job** (retail stores, restaurants, business services, administrative, etc.). Try to find a position in a field you genuinely like. If you enjoy shopping or love the products of a particular store, consider working in retail. If you have a passion for cooking or are knowledgeable about food, you might want to be a prep chef at a favorite restaurant. If you have connections at business service organizations and can add value to their operations, try working at a company where your managerial contributions would be valued. Contact several temp agencies, or go visit businesses in which you have an interest.

- **Teaching or substitute teaching** (public or private schools, colleges and universities, technical or vocational programs, etc.). The education that helped get you started in your career is still valuable. If you've been in the workforce for a while, you've no doubt gained skills to enhance your credibility. These qualifications are often valued by schools and colleges. Experienced professionals are sought after to teach classes and bring a real-world perspective to their students. Contact the administration office of your local school system or the employment office of universities and vocational programs in your area.
- **Consulting or contract assignments** (business operations, computer/technology, creative/advertising, etc.). Even before the economy and job market went sour, the work world had changed. A growing percentage of the workforce had already moved into flexible assignments as consultants or contractors. If you have a background in one of the fields that naturally lend themselves to this work style, try to get consulting or contract work. It can be interesting, challenging work, and it can also be lucrative. In some cases, these consulting or contract assignments turn into full-time job offers, after the company gets to know you. Contact outsourcing and contract employment firms in the fields that interest you.
- **Work for family or friends** (retail stores, services, small manufacturing operations, and every other type of business). Do you have relatives or friends who own or run businesses? Would you be comfortable working with them? In tough times, it is important to put your pride aside and ask for help. But in this case, the help would be mutual. Your friend or relative would be the lucky recipient of your services, and you would be gainfully employed, working for someone you already know and like. Contact every friend, relative, or acquaintance who owns or runs a business, and ask about their needs and challenges.

- **Home-based work** (administrative, sales, computer work, creative assignments, bookkeeping, personal services, etc.). With the advent of the Internet and computers, it is easier than ever to do real work from home. Some of this work can be enjoyable and lucrative. There is no longer a stigma about working from home, and in fact, you may find that the flexible, independent lifestyle suits you. From copywriting to doing proposals to preparing tax returns, there's no limit to the options. Ask yourself what skills you have, and offer your services to appropriate companies and families in your area. Contact everyone in your network to offer your services and ask for referrals.
- **Odd jobs** (handyman, construction, painting, moving and hauling, yard work, plowing, etc.). Are you handy around the house? Do you have special equipment or tools? Do you have trade skills that you could offer to other people in your town? There is always a need for reliable, professional help in these areas. If you're not afraid to get your hands dirty, you can earn good money providing these much-needed services to organizations and individuals. Contact everyone in your network to offer your services, and be sure to ask for referrals.

18. Why You Can't Afford *Not* to Have a Strategic Plan

If you're serious about getting a job when no one's hiring, you'll need more than determination, a strong mindset, and a dash of luck; you'll need a strategy and a system to implement that strategy. The Career Potential℠ coaching process I use with my private clients involves five distinct phases. But to make it even easier to understand this model, you can distill your strategic plan into two fundamental stages:

- **Preparation and Research.** You'll handle these phases primarily on your own or with a career coach. They involve introspective exercises, research, thinking, writing, planning, and the creation of your Job Search Survival Toolkit. This stage is an inside job.
- **Implementation and Activity**. You'll be out in the real world, contacting new people, networking, having meetings, talking with recruiters, interviewing, negotiating, and ultimately landing a new position. This stage of the work is the outside job.

This book is designed to help you get clear on your desired career path, create the best possible set of job search tools, and implement a productive and successful job search campaign. That's what we're about to embark upon—with you as the client and me as your Virtual Career Coach.

Haphazard job search activity without a strategic plan is nothing more than a recipe for disappointment and a prolonged period of career pain. With the economy and job market in a tailspin, we want to get you headed in the right direction and fully employed as soon as possible. Ready? Then let's get to work!

> You'll need more than determination, a strong mindset, and a dash of luck; you'll need a strategy and a system to implement that strategy.

19. In a Bad Job Market, You Must Work Backward to Reach Your Goals

You want to take charge of your career, find a job you love, and earn what you deserve. Sounds good, but it can be difficult to know where to start, especially in a tough job market. There are usually conflicting thoughts and feelings involved, and too often, the result is a kind of paralysis. In addition, most people simply lack the necessary resources, knowledge, and skills to conduct an effective job search campaign on their own, especially when no one's hiring.

Although finding a better job or a more satisfying career might feel like a very random and confusing experience, through this book, you'll learn the strategies you need to consistently produce excellent results.

20. Career Success Is an Inside Job

We need to go back and start at the beginning. That means doing an internal audit of yourself. As I often tell my clients, career development is an inside game. We go inside before we look outside. If you want to achieve your career potential, you must first get totally clear on such questions as who you are, what's important to you, what you really want and need, what your long-term goals are, what motivates you, what your professional preferences are, and more.

Only after you've gained clarity on these issues does it makes sense to go out into the world and manifest your own unique vision of career success. Getting into resumes, interviewing, negotiating, networking, and all the other typical job search topics before you've laid a strong foundation will only create frenzied activity without forward movement. Perhaps you've already experienced this. It can be very frustrating, depressing, and—worst of all—demotivating. As you work through the strategies and use the tools in this part of the book, keep in mind the following words of career wisdom:

> People don't succeed by migrating to a "hot" industry or by adopting a particular career-guiding mantra. They thrive by focusing on the question of who they really are, and connecting that to the work they truly love. The choice isn't about a career search so much as an identity quest.
>
> —Po Bronson, *What Should I Do With My Life?*

21. The Start at the Beginning Strategy

To get your job search started on the right foot, it's important to build a solid foundation of self-knowledge and clarity. The exercises and questions on the following pages will help you clarify some of the issues and values that are fundamental to your lasting career success. They'll also provide you with a uniquely personalized set of keys to unlock the door to a great job, even when no one's hiring.

It may seem to you that doing these exercises during a job market crisis will just delay the launch of your search. You may even feel that such introspection is a waste of time. If this is true for you, I urge you to reconsider. After working with thousands of clients in transition, I have seen consistent evidence that these exercises actually accelerate my clients' progress and get them to their career destinations much faster. I assure you that the time and effort you invest in these exercises will pay off in many multiples.

Exercise: Values Clarification (Downloadable)

Rank the following values on a scale of 1 through 10, with 1 representing "Not important to me at all" and 10 representing "Very important to me." The context of these questions is "your whole life" (personal, family, professional, community), and not just your work or career.

Collaboration/Teamwork	1 - 2 - 3 - 4 - 5 - 6 - 7 - 8 - 9 - 10
Management/Leadership	1 - 2 - 3 - 4 - 5 - 6 - 7 - 8 - 9 - 10
Money/Wealth	1 - 2 - 3 - 4 - 5 - 6 - 7 - 8 - 9 - 10
Security/Safety	1 - 2 - 3 - 4 - 5 - 6 - 7 - 8 - 9 - 10
Adventure/Discovery	1 - 2 - 3 - 4 - 5 - 6 - 7 - 8 - 9 - 10
Independence/Freedom	1 - 2 - 3 - 4 - 5 - 6 - 7 - 8 - 9 - 10
Control People/Projects	1 - 2 - 3 - 4 - 5 - 6 - 7 - 8 - 9 - 10
Life Balance	1 - 2 - 3 - 4 - 5 - 6 - 7 - 8 - 9 - 10
Friendship/Camaraderie	1 - 2 - 3 - 4 - 5 - 6 - 7 - 8 - 9 - 10
Recognition/Acknowledgment	1 - 2 - 3 - 4 - 5 - 6 - 7 - 8 - 9 - 10
Fun/Enjoyment	1 - 2 - 3 - 4 - 5 - 6 - 7 - 8 - 9 - 10
Achievement/Accomplishment	1 - 2 - 3 - 4 - 5 - 6 - 7 - 8 - 9 - 10
Power/Influence	1 - 2 - 3 - 4 - 5 - 6 - 7 - 8 - 9 - 10
Logic/Analysis	1 - 2 - 3 - 4 - 5 - 6 - 7 - 8 - 9 - 10
Service/Contribution	1 - 2 - 3 - 4 - 5 - 6 - 7 - 8 - 9 - 10
Challenge/Overcoming Obstacles	1 - 2 - 3 - 4 - 5 - 6 - 7 - 8 - 9 - 10
Creativity/Innovation	1 - 2 - 3 - 4 - 5 - 6 - 7 - 8 - 9 - 10
Technical Competency	1 - 2 - 3 - 4 - 5 - 6 - 7 - 8 - 9 - 10
Health/Wellness	1 - 2 - 3 - 4 - 5 - 6 - 7 - 8 - 9 - 10
Kindness/Generosity	1 - 2 - 3 - 4 - 5 - 6 - 7 - 8 - 9 - 10
Education/Knowledge	1 - 2 - 3 - 4 - 5 - 6 - 7 - 8 - 9 - 10

To download this element of your Job Search Survival Toolkit, visit: www.CareerPotential.com/bookbonus.

Special Note: Above is the first reference to this web link: **www.CareerPotential.com/bookbonus.** You'll see this link many times throughout the rest of the book. Visiting this web page gives you instant access to "Your Job Search Survival Toolkit, " which includes a whole array of downloadable examples, exercises, and forms. These interactive resources will make it much easier for you to develop your own "Toolkit," and they'll also save you an enormous amount of time and effort. Be sure to take full advantage of these value-added, online elements of the book, all of which are designed to help you get the job you want, even when no one's hiring.

Exercise: Birds of a Feather (Downloadable)

Complete the sentences on this page. Work fairly quickly, writing what comes most readily to mind, without overthinking.

1. In my free time, the activities or hobbies I like to do most are...

   ___

   ___

2. Whenever I go to a bookstore, the section(s) I always seem to be drawn to are...

   ___

   ___

3. My closest friends work in the following fields, businesses, and professions...

   ___

   ___

4. The kind(s) of environments I usually feel most comfortable working in are...

   ___

   ___

5. My friends (or colleagues, acquaintances, family members) have often told me that I should be a...

   ___

   ___

6. The things that have always motivated me most are...

   ___

   ___

7. I have often been praised for my work in...

___

___

8. If I were to get involved in volunteer work (unpaid), I'd like to work in...

___

___

When you're finished and satisfied with your answers, focus on the two vital questions below. Write down your thoughts in as much detail as possible.

(a) What does this tell me about my core values and interests, and my motivational patterns?

___

___

(b) What implications do these answers have on my current and future career choices?

___

___

To download this element of your Job Search Survival Toolkit, visit: www.CareerPotential.com/bookbonus.

Exercise: Your Original Joys (Downloadable)

Think back as far as possible, to when you were very young. Let your mind wander freely, without editing, especially to the private, special times when you were allowed to play or daydream or do whatever you wanted. Recall the kinds of interests you had and activities you pursued in those early years.

What did you love? What fascinated you? What senses did you live through most, or did you enjoy them all equally? What did you daydream about, no matter how silly or unimportant it may seem now? What were the secrets and little games you never told any

(*Continued*)

body about? What could you lose yourself in and be very happy? What kinds of things gave you greatest pleasure?

List five to ten items below that match the criteria above:

1. ______________________________
2. ______________________________
3. ______________________________
4. ______________________________
5. ______________________________
6. ______________________________
7. ______________________________
8. ______________________________
9. ______________________________
10. ______________________________

Put a star next to three of the items you've written that were most meaningful or special to you. Write down your thoughts about why these particular ones stand out.

To download this element of your Job Search Survival Toolkit, visit: www.CareerPotential.com/bookbonus.

Example: Passions and Gifts

Passions and Gifts is a wonderful exercise to get you focused on the larger purpose of all your work. It connects you to your WHY and is a great tool to help sharpen your delivery during networking meetings and interviews. You'll see a completed example of this exercise below, done by one of my clients.

I am passionate about...

Doing the impossible, taking on big challenges

Creating new structures to achieve big results

Solving problems, removing obstacles

Getting the best out of people

I really like. . .

Working with very bright people who have good values

Working with companies that are respected or where respect can be created

Building a culture that will succeed and be a place where people can grow and enjoy work

My greatest contribution is. . .

Being able to do many different things well

Accomplishing the mission, exceeding expectations

Building an organization from scratch

Saving the day—taking dire situations, fixing them, and turning them into winners

I am particularly good at. . .

Taking things that look like failures and making them into exceptional successes

Developing people—getting them to be creative, committed, and accountable

Getting the job done quickly with practical, interesting solutions

I am known for. . .

Creative leadership

Overcoming challenging obstacles

Rising to the occasion

Seeing the core issues, problems, solutions

Getting to the heart of the matter quickly, and intuitively analyzing the situation

I have exceptional ability to. . .

Devise straightforward solutions that are efficient and practical

Take complex problems and quickly develop elegant solutions

Create solutions that get the job done

(*Continued*)

Exercise: Passions and Gifts (Downloadable)

Now it's your turn. Complete the following sentences. You may list multiple answers for each of the items below. Keep your responses focused on the career and work aspects of your life.

I feel passionate about...

What I really like is...

My greatest contribution is...

I am particularly good at...

I am known for...

I have an exceptional ability to...

Colleagues often ask for my help with...

What motivates me most is...

I would feel disappointed, frustrated, or sad if I couldn't do...

Now that you have completed this Passions and Gifts exercise, ask yourself these important questions. Write down your answers in detail.

1. Do your passions and gifts correspond/align with your current career direction?

   ____

   ____

   ____

   ____

2. What implications do these answers have on your current and future career choices?

   ____

   ____

   ____

   ____

3. What is one thing you can do right now to enhance or change your current career situation for the better?

   ____

   ____

   ____

   ____

Remember: Regardless of external circumstances, you always have the opportunity to take charge of your career and find the work you love—as long as you have the right resources and support.

To download this element of your Job Search Survival Toolkit, visit: www.CareerPotential.com/bookbonus.

Regardless of external circumstances, you always have the opportunity to take charge of your career and find the work you love—as long as you have the right resources and support.

22. The Dream Job Strategy

When you were very young, what kind of work seemed like the most fun? What did you dream of being when you grew up? What were your ideal careers?

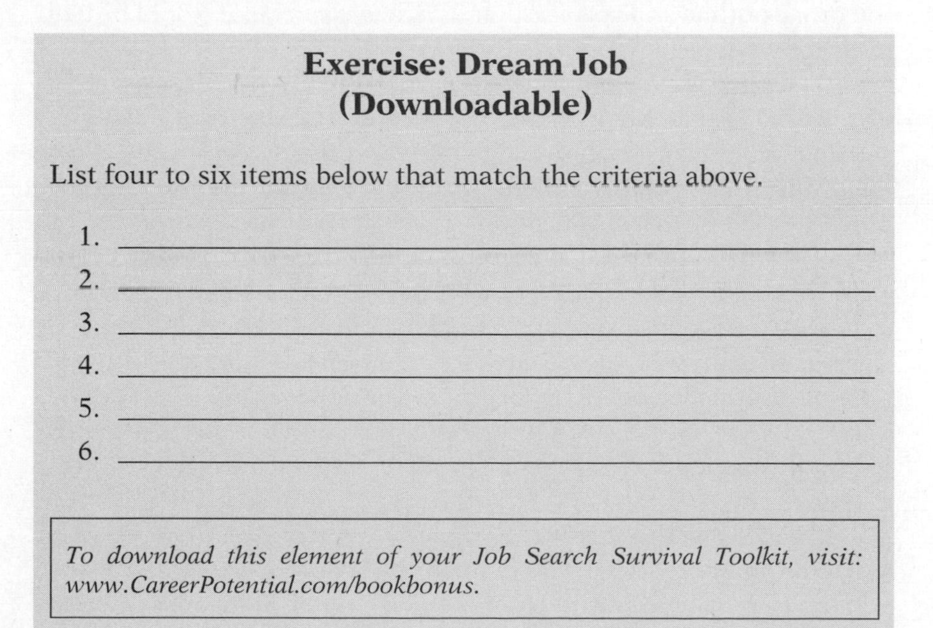

Exercise: Dream Job (Downloadable)

List four to six items below that match the criteria above.

1. ____________________
2. ____________________
3. ____________________
4. ____________________
5. ____________________
6. ____________________

To download this element of your Job Search Survival Toolkit, visit: www.CareerPotential.com/bookbonus.

Put a star next to three of these items that were most meaningful, enjoyable, or special to you. Write down your thoughts about why these particular ones stand out.

23. The Ideal Workday Strategy

This is a very powerful and personal exercise, which will help you explore and then clearly define what an ideal workday looks and feels like, and how you might experience it on a moment-by-moment basis. Once you've vividly imagined the details of this day on paper, you'll be much better prepared to create it for yourself in real life.

Read over the following example and then take at least one hour of quiet time to write down *your* ideal workday. Your aim should be to create as much detail as you need to generate a clear and specific picture in your mind of the day's events, activities, people, environments, schedules, structures—and your experiences of each of these factors.

So block out some time and put some real energy into this exercise. Take a relaxing hot bath, go for a walk in the park, sit under a tree, enjoy a glass of wine by the fireplace. Do whatever it takes to visit that inner place where you can reflect and really imagine both the broad outline and specific details of a workday that would be truly *ideal* for *you*!

The purpose of this exercise is to elicit the qualitative aspects of a work life that would create the best fit and the most day-to-day satisfaction for you—acknowledging the fact that not *every* day can be ideal, but that in an overall sense, this would be the best possible outcome of your career transition.

The main point of this exercise is that you must first get crystal clear on *exactly* what your ideal workday would look like, if you hope to later manifest this experience in the real world. Generally speaking, the job you really want is not out there in some newspaper ad or Internet posting, waiting for you to find it. Your ideal opportunity is best defined inside of you, but you won't be able to create it—or even recognize it—until you can develop this laser focus on your next job or future career.

I realize that this might be a whole new way of looking at things for you, but I guarantee that if you jump in and give your all to this exercise, you'll see amazing things start to happen to your job search or career transition.

You must first get crystal clear on *exactly* what your ideal workday would look like, if you hope to later manifest this experience in the real world.

Here's an example of an Ideal Workday exercise, which was recently completed by a client of mine:

Example: Ideal Workday

From 6:15 A.M. to 8:30 A.M.: In my ideal workday, I wake up at 6:15 a.m., cuddle for a while with Sandy, get out of bed, dress in sneakers, shorts, and a T-shirt, do some push-ups and sit-ups, stretch. and go for a 30-minute jog. I run along the streets of my town, stopping to say hello to my neighbors and pet their dog. I return to my house and make and drink a banana milkshake while I brew a cup of coffee for Sandy and a cup for myself, and listen to the morning news on NPR. I take coffee to Sandy in bed, shave, take a shower, get dressed, eat some cereal and yogurt, read the paper, and get out the door by 8:00 A.M.

I dress in stylish, well-made, professional-looking clothes. I walk 20 minutes to work in the sunshine and a cool breeze, stopping off at the coffee shop on the ground floor of the building my office is in to fill my Thermos with coffee for the first half of the day, and maybe grab a toasted bagel.

I have my own office just off the main work area on our floor, surrounded by the cubicles of the six people—two designers, two copywriters, and a creative director—who report to me. My office has a frosted-glass-and-copper desk, a window, good lighting, a chair that's good for my posture, a couple of chairs for guests, a few plants, an original modern art painting by my friend on the wall, a metal bookshelf, a few photos, and a laptop connected to a large flat-panel monitor.

From 8:30 A.M. to 8:55 A.M.: I review my plans for the day and week, read and respond to e-mail from my team, customers, and other senior management, and make any phone calls I need to. I check on ongoing projects; provide feedback, guidance, and motivation to my team; and help out colleagues or customers who are

(*Continued*)

turning to me as a subject-matter expert. Once an hour during the day, I walk from my desk to the water cooler near the front desk for a stretch, a glass of water, and to look out in the distance over the city.

From 9:00 A.M. to 9:50 A.M.: I have a conference call with the United Kingdom office to help plan their weekly presentations and schedule a few meetings with strategic account prospects. I squeeze in some conversation about traveling in the United Kingdom, as Sandy will be flying over at the start of her break in classes, and we'll be seeing friends of mine in England for three days before traveling for two weeks in Ireland.

From 10:00 A.M. to 10:50 A.M.: I work on my presentation. I'm preparing notes from conversations I've had with customers about the headaches and challenges of creating solutions like this, and demonstrating how we can make the headaches and challenges go away. I'm incorporating a new type of software, so I'm practicing working with it, using it to add some flash and drama to the presentation. I e-mail the presentation to our account executives, asking them to let me know their reactions and any questions that come up.

From 11:00 A.M. to 11:30 A.M.: I participate in a conference call with one of our national account managers. He is working with a client who has extensive marketing needs, and wants to be reassured that our company has sufficient expertise to help them. Our account executive and I have prepared in advance for this meeting, and I have supplied him with a likely set of questions the client will ask based on my prior experience. In addition, I've got our designer in the office with me, because he can help and he wants to learn more about the sales process.

As our national account manager leads the meeting, I have the speakerphone muted and am running a commentary on what he's saying, the techniques he's using, and the way he guides the meeting to the conclusion he's looking for. He successfully answers four out of five of the potential client's questions, and when he asks me about the last one, I make a joke out of thanking him for letting me feel useful, and answer the question to everyone's satisfaction. The call ends, and I debrief with our designer to answer any remaining questions and wrap up the session.

From 12:00 noon to 12:30 P.M.: I walk from the office to the park, enjoying the sunshine and the sights and sounds of the city (while eating the sandwich Sandy made and packed for me while I was out jogging).

From 12:30 P.M. to 12:45 P.M.: I stop in at the restaurant where a number of our clients are, and drink a cup of coffee while I welcome them into our organization, connect with them, and explain that if they have any ideas about the campaign they would like to see us incorporate, they should feel free to contact me, as I champion new ideas at our company.

From 12:45 P.M. to 1:15 P.M.: I run a brown-bag luncheon training class for the staff on creative selling techniques and doing powerful presentations.

From 1:15 P.M. to 1:30 P.M.: I respond to e-mails and recheck my progress on the day. I'm doing well, accomplishing what I want to accomplish.

From 1:30 P.M. to 2:15 P.M.: I talk with our national account director about the tools and skills that will enable our sales force to achieve maximum productivity and present the most polished image to our current and prospective clients. We also review a demonstration reel I developed for one of our new accounts, and I make some notes on feedback that salespeople have provided about the demo, as well as feedback clients and prospects have provided. I make a note in my calendar to work with one of our designers to update the reel tomorrow.

From 2:00 P.M. to 2:45 P.M.: I meet with my designers, copywriters, and creative director. We talk about creative concepts and brainstorm ideas about how we can use any new techniques to our advantage, either to maintain a cutting-edge image for our agency, or to incorporate into our presentations.

From 2:45 P.M. to 3:30 P.M.: I work on a small design assignment that is pro bono. Although we won't make a dime on it, it just may help us win a significant deal with another organization. I complete it and then forward it on to my creative director for his input. Tomorrow, I'll put together a 10-slide presentation that will be shown to the nonprofit client some time next week via WebEx and teleconference.

From 3:30 P.M. to 4:45 P.M.: I write and respond to e-mails, make a few phone calls, and do a final check on my progress for the day. I did well. I accomplished nearly everything I wanted to, and the things that remain are things I'm looking forward to doing tomorrow.

4:45 P.M.: I leave the office and walk home. I've got a real sense of accomplishment and a story or two I can tell Sandy about my day in a way that will interest her. I'm looking forward to giving her a solid idea of what I did today and how I enjoyed it.

(*Continued*)

Now that you've seen a good example of the Ideal Workday exercise, it's time for you to try it! Remember to provide as much detail as you possibly can in designing your ideal workday. Use your imagination, and have *fun* with this one.

24. The Stepping Stone Strategy

The following questions form the stepping stones that will lead you in the right direction when deciding your next career move. Sometimes, answering life's large questions can be a daunting task, whereas answering smaller questions along the way, with purpose and clarity, can reveal your path in a clearer, more manageable, and less overwhelming manner.

Answering smaller questions along the way, with purpose and clarity, can reveal your path in a clearer, more manageable, and less overwhelming manner.

Try it now. Write down your answers to the following questions in as much detail as possible. Try not to skip ahead, and give each question enough thought to generate a complete answer without feeling that your answers need to be final. The process is more important than the final document, which you can always revisit and revise. Be as thorough and candid as possible, and take as much time as you need.

Exercise: Stepping Stone Strategy (Downloadable)

- Describe your current career situation as succinctly as possible; include both the good and the bad.

____
____
____
____

- Describe the way you would *ideally* like it to be. Be as specific as possible in identifying your primary career desires.

____

____

____

____

- What are you doing in your work that you want to continue doing? With whom?

____

____

____

____

- Does anyone else you know now have the kind of work situation you envision? If so, describe it in detail. What steps did this person take to get there?

____

____

____

____

- What is necessary for your future (goals) regarding money, time, and quality of life—in one year? Five years? Ten years?

____

____

____

____

- What are you *not* doing professionally that you would like to be doing?

____

____

____

____

- What *unique* qualities or characteristics do you bring to your career?

____

____

____

____

(*Continued*)

- In your work, what skills and abilities are *not* being properly utilized or fully expressed?

- What predictable blocks (organizational, personal, emotional, financial, etc.) might prevent you from reaching your goals?

- What might you lose or leave behind if you were to make a significant career change, for a better situation? (personal, practical, emotional, financial, status, etc.)

- Do you know what your career goal or objective is (short-term and long-term)? If so, have you written it down?

- What is the primary motivator/driver in your career? Has this been consistent, or has it changed?

- How will you know when you're on the right track? When you've arrived?

To download this element of your Job Search Survival Toolkit, visit: www.CareerPotential.com/bookbonus.

25. From Exploration to Execution

Having gone through the preliminary internal exercises, it's time to brainstorm some logical options, and then narrow down the possibilities to a carefully-thought-out list of initial career options and job choices. From your exploration and reflection on the previous pages, start to eliminate the pipe dreams and focus on the opportunities that fit best with your strengths, experience, and preferences. For example, if you always wanted to be a fighter pilot, but you've spent the last 20 years as an accountant, then maybe going to work as a financial executive for a major airline headquartered in your city would make more sense than climbing into a cockpit.

Make your initial cut by sitting down and writing out a list of possible careers or jobs that are a realistic fit with what you've learned about yourself. Then develop some related options, perhaps with the help of a relative or close friend. Solicit market feedback from former colleagues, associates, and other professionals who are in a position to know both your skills and the requirements of your target positions.

Solicit market feedback from former colleagues, associates, and other professionals who are in a position to know both your skills and the requirements of your target positions.

Then do some research on what is required to enter that field. If all signs point to a good fit, then mobilize your resources, get into action, and go after those opportunities.

26. Excellent Tools to Help You Get a Job When No One's Hiring

There are some great tools and resources you can use to help you identify appropriate career paths and job roles. Many people are unaware of them or simply do not make the effort to track them down. When no one's hiring, these tools can make all the difference between you becoming a career victor—or a career victim. The following resources are often as close as your nearest public library, university, newsstand, or convention center:

- Library research (visit the business department of the largest library in your area)
- Dictionary of Holland Occupational Codes

- Occupational Outlook Handbook, U.S. Department of Labor
- Professional associations and organizations
- Free and low-cost career seminars and professional development programs
- Online employment and business databases
- Trade magazines, books, newsletters, and blogs
- Industry-specific networking functions
- Business conferences and expos
- Job fairs

27. Narrowing Your Choices Is Easier Than You Think

Although narrowing your choices is a very personal process—and leads to very important career decisions—it can be boiled down to three basic steps:

1. Identify the *consistent themes* from all the preliminary exercises.
2. Create an *employer wish list* that includes all of the characteristics of an ideal company to work for.
3. Create the *dream job description* that matches the criteria you discovered in the preliminary exercises.

28. The Employer Wish List Strategy

The time has come to create a wish list of adjectives that describe your ideal employer, such as size, location, industry, culture, values, environment, people, revenue, etc. When no one's hiring, you may be tempted to shorten this process down to "my wish list is for an employer who gives out paychecks," but you would be shortchanging yourself in a big way. Let me state again that in tough economic times, it pays to be laser-focused on exactly what you're after. Don't hold back! This is *your* fantasy, so list what you would really *love* in the next company you work for.

> In tough economic times, it pays to be laser-focused on exactly what you're after.

If you don't know what you want most in an employer, how will you know when you've found the right one? Or, as the TV personality Dr. Phil McGraw is fond of saying: "You've got to name it before you can claim it!"

Here is one example of an Employer Wish List, which was completed by one of my clients:

Example: Employer Wish List

Physical

- Downtown location, or less than 30 minutes commute via train
- 50 to 100 employees
- Upscale physical environment
- U.S. company with international operations, customers, or sales
- Headquarters office of corporation

Intellectual

- Good three-year plan with strategic growth as primary driver
- Solid financial skills common at top management level
- Solid strategic skills common at top management level

Performance

- Revenues of $2.5M to $5M
- Growing in revenues
- Ranked top five in industry by revenue
- Diverse customer base
- High revenue per customer (at least $10,000 annually)

Culture

- High professional standards
- Informal but polished and mature atmosphere
- Business to business, high casual dress code
- Diverse workforce

(*Continued*)

- Fast-paced but sane environment
- Focused on working hard on a standard schedule (not working all the time)

Social

- Nonharmful industry (no tobacco, firearms, etc.)
- Progressive benefits policy
- Active community involvement
- People who enjoy their work and work hard, but have other priorities

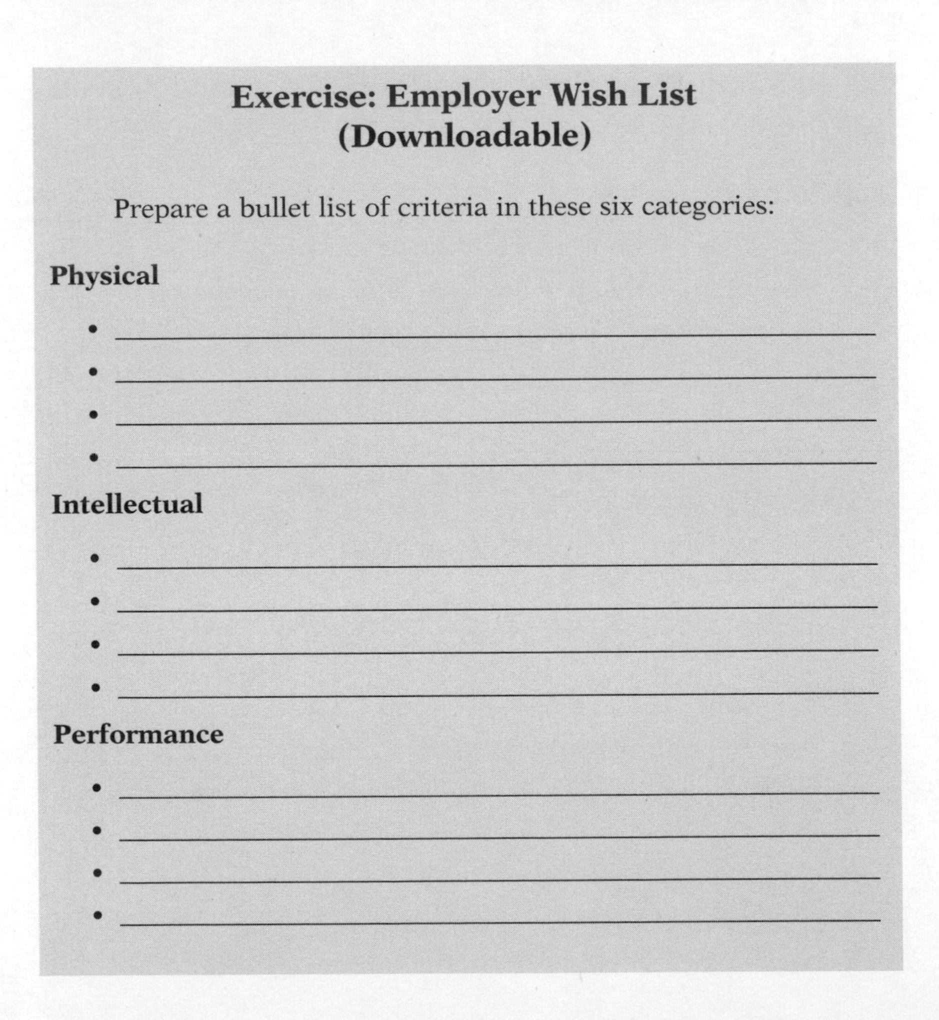

Exercise: Employer Wish List (Downloadable)

Prepare a bullet list of criteria in these six categories:

Physical

- ______________________________
- ______________________________
- ______________________________
- ______________________________

Intellectual

- ______________________________
- ______________________________
- ______________________________
- ______________________________

Performance

- ______________________________
- ______________________________
- ______________________________
- ______________________________

Cultural

- ______________________________
- ______________________________
- ______________________________
- ______________________________

Social

- ______________________________
- ______________________________
- ______________________________
- ______________________________

Other

- ______________________________
- ______________________________
- ______________________________
- ______________________________

To download this element of your Job Search Survival Toolkit, visit: www.CareerPotential.com/bookbonus.

29. You Must Be Crystal Clear on Your Perfect Job Before It Can Become a Reality

When no one's hiring, you might be thinking, "I can't wait around for my perfect job. I just need to get *any* job." But remember, that approach will almost always prove to be shortsighted and self-defeating. If you get focused on the job you'd really *love*, you'll be much closer to landing a good job that will move your career in the right direction.

If you get focused on the job you'd really *love*, you'll be much closer to landing a good job that will move your career in the right direction.

Now it's time to draft your own perfect job description. Here's your big chance to finally design the job you've always wanted. Be bold! Use your imagination! Do some research, surf the Web, go through your old employment files, read the help-wanted ads. Do whatever you need to do in order to create what you would truly call a perfect job for you at this point in your career.

Example: Perfect Job Description

Title: Director of Real Estate Operations

Position Overview: This is an outstanding opportunity to join a rapidly growing retailer with a plan for national expansion. We are looking for a real estate professional who can manage the entire real estate project life cycle, including site selection, lease negotiations, design/development, construction, and maintenance.

Reporting Relationships & Responsibilities:

- This position reports directly to the VP of Operations.
- This position has the following direct reports: real estate coordinator, two real estate managers, construction manager, and an administrative assistant.

Requirements & Qualifications:

- Exceptional communication skills and ability to lead project teams to meet critical deadlines.
- Expert in negotiating leases and construction contracts.
- Innovative individual who can create new ideas for cost reduction.
- Manage complex budgets for new store construction, existing store renovation, and facility management.

Roles & Responsibilities:

- Prepare site selection packages including demographics, market data, maps, aerials, photographs, competitive information, traffic counts, and sales information.

- Facilitate and coordinate with local developers to gain approvals, including attending entitlement and other meetings, and manage the outcome of those meetings to all extents possible to ensure that our best interests are protected while still moving projects forward.
- Complete contracts for architectural work, construction, and major maintenance.
- Complete project budgets, change orders, and turnkey cost additions as required.
- Manage architects, engineers, and general contractors to ensure the project is of good quality, is completed on time, and is completed within the budget.
- Support all operating stores with regard to technical issues and problems or project requests.

Compensation:

- $110,000 annual base salary, bonuses tied to achieving number of new store openings and target open dates.
- Potential for ownership/equity.
- Cell phone and auto allowance, four weeks of vacation, 401K with 100 percent match, telecommuting option.
- Premium insurance plan for health/dental/vision with low copay (under $100 per month).

Exercise: Perfect Job Description (Downloadable)

Draft your own perfect job description, outlining your criteria in the following seven sections:

Title: ______________________________

____

____

____

(*Continued*)

Position Overview: ______________________________

____

____

____

Reporting Relationships & Responsibilities: ______________

____

____

____

Requirements & Qualifications: ____________________

____

____

____

Roles & Responsibilities: ________________________

____

____

____

Compensation: ________________________________

____

____

____

Other Criteria: _______________________________

____

____

____

To download this element of your Job Search Survival Toolkit, visit: www.CareerPotential.com/bookbonus.

PART III

Leveraging Your Core Job Seeker Materials

30. The Best Tools Get the Best Jobs, Especially in a Down Market

A photographer would never show up for a fashion shoot with just one camera lens. A carpenter would never arrive at a construction site with only a hammer. An artist would never apply for a design position without showing a complete portfolio of samples. So why do most job seekers use only their resume as the cornerstone of their search? This is not effective under ordinary circumstances, and it's absolutely deadly if you're trying to get a job when no one's hiring.

In this section of the book, we'll do the bulk of the work on preparing your complete arsenal of career success documents, otherwise known as your Job Search Survival Toolkit.

31. Surprise: Your Resume Is Your *Least* Important Tool

Here's something you may find hard to believe, but it's critically important to your job search success: your resume should be your least-used job search tool. If you're interested in finding a new job in a tough employment market, you've probably been thinking a lot about your resume. You've undoubtedly looked at sample resumes, struggled with wording, and talked with friends who have recently been through career transitions. But your anxiety may be based on incorrect assumptions.

Most job seekers use their resume as the centerpiece of their entire search. But the resume should actually be one of your *least-used* job-seeking tools. The fact is that resumes should spend most of their time in your computer, in briefcases, or in desk drawers—not spread around like so much confetti.

Resumes should spend most of their time in your computer, in briefcases, or in desk drawers—not spread around like so much confetti.

So, why write a resume in the first place? The main reason is to improve your thinking, so you'll be better prepared to market yourself as the standout candidate when no one's hiring. Writing a resume mentally prepares you for career success. It forces you to take stock of where you've been, where you are, where you want to go, and how to reach your goals. Once you've gone through this thinking process, the resume itself almost becomes an afterthought.

In fact, only four circumstances call for the use of a resume: (1) answering a help-wanted ad or Internet job posting, (2) supplying a copy upon request to a prospective employer or recruiter who has an appropriate opening, (3) posting it on career opportunity web sites, and (4) giving it to selected recruiters at job fairs.

If you're distributing copies of your resume at other times, STOP! You're probably overemphasizing the resume because your other job-seeking tools—the ones that make a real difference when the economy is down—are weak or nonexistent.

32. Survival of the Fittest Is the Law of the Job Search Jungle

Darwin's law of natural selection is based on the phrase "survival of the fittest." Most people associate this concept with lions and tigers, because they are commonly thought to be the strongest animals in the jungle and the fiercest predators. However, fittest does not mean strongest; it means most adaptable to change.

So if the markets are melting down, if financial turmoil is everywhere, and if jobless claims are hitting record highs, it doesn't matter how strong you are; it only matters how adaptable, flexible, and savvy you are in navigating the new employment landscape. Part of being adaptable is having a complete portfolio of career tools. The goal is to use the *right* tool at the *right* time for the *right* purpose with the *right* person. Mastering this approach will help you to not only survive, but *thrive*, in your job search.

We'll get into a lot more detail on each of these tools, but for now, let's review your core job seeker materials.

1. **Written Accomplishments.** Write five or six stories about work-related tasks that made you proud. Describe the challenge or problem, your specific actions, and the positive results you produced. These stories can be from any time in your career and any job you've had. These are usually examples of times when you exceeded the scope of your job's responsibilities. Don't worry, I'll show you exactly how to create these, and there are *lots* of examples coming up.
2. **Verbal Presentations.** Prepare and practice a Positioning Statement (also known as a 30-second commercial) about who you are professionally, the industries you've served, and the particular strengths you can contribute to a new employer. When you write it out, keep it brief, and then memorize it so it will always be on the tip of your tongue. You'll also need a Departure Statement, a prepared explanation of why you're no longer with your previous employer, or why you're seeking a new position (even if you're still working). Details on how to craft your specific Positioning and Departure statements are coming up later.
3. **Professional Biography.** Write a one-page narrative of your career in the third person—as though someone else wrote it about you. This is no time to be modest, so make it sound impressive. This will be the primary tool you'll use in all of your networking. Somewhere in the middle of the document, create a bullet list of the tangible results you have achieved (which are drawn directly from your accomplishment stories.) Step-by-step details and plenty of examples follow later.
4. **Target Company List.** Make a wish list of adjectives that would describe your ideal employer, such as size, location, industry, culture, values, environment, people, and so on. Then research specific organizations that meet those criteria. Create separate folders for each of these companies, and gather as much information as you can. Prepare a list of these organizations, categorized by industry. You'll eventually network your way in to meet with the hiring managers (not Human Resources) at these

companies. Complete details on how to assemble this list can be found later.

5. **Contact List.** Compile a list of all the people you know personally and professionally. Yes, *all* of them! Include their names, phone numbers, and e-mail addresses. Don't edit the list or make any assumptions about who can or can't help you. The fact is that approximately 80 percent of new opportunities are secured through networking, and a very high percentage of those positions were discovered through people who were *least* expected to be of help. Your list should number in the hundreds.
6. **Professional References.** List colleagues who would sing your praises if asked about you. Contact each of them, and get approval to use their names on your list of references. Be sure to provide these individuals with guidance about what to say when prospective employers call. Also, ask these references to contact you immediately when prospective employers call them. I'll give you several reference strategies later.
7. **Letters of Recommendation.** Request letters from four or five respected business associates, printed on their company letterhead (if they can't or won't use corporate letterhead, personal letterhead will suffice). These individuals could be superiors, subordinates, peers, suppliers, clients, vendors, and so forth. Try to mix it up with individuals from various companies and in several different roles. I'll show you exactly how to request these letters and also what sorts of things they should contain.
8. **Networking Script.** People often find it difficult to get started with their networking because they feel nervous or afraid of making a mistake. The best way to avoid this problem is to learn the specific steps (the agenda) of a networking discussion—how it flows, what to expect, how to react to the other person's comments, and so on. In addition, it is smart to write out a full script so you'll know exactly what to say and how to say it. By preparing this networking script in advance, you'll feel much more confident and productive in networking. We'll walk through this together, and you'll become comfortable to the point that your presentation will sound natural, compelling, and real—not "canned."
9. **Tracking System.** Keep a detailed record in hard copy of your job search activities, including phone calls, meeting notes, correspondence, and follow-up steps. This is vital for planning and

assessing your performance from week to week. Use preprinted forms, folders, software programs, and other means of staying organized. I have included some suggested templates, which you can adapt for your own use.

10. **Resume.** Make no mistake. You *do* need a resume, and it has to be great. But it really should be the least-used tool in your portfolio.

By integrating all 10 of these documents and tools into your job search—and not relying solely on your resume—you'll add power, professionalism, and flexibility to your efforts. It may take some time to produce these documents and to learn how to use them effectively, but it will be worth it. Getting a great job when no one's hiring is *much easier* when you have the right tools.

Now is the time to create a complete portfolio of job search tools to market yourself as the standout candidate who companies can't afford *not* to hire.

> Getting a great job when no one's hiring is much easier when you have the right tools.

For the rest of this section, you'll be collecting all of the ingredients for—and assembling step-by-step—the core components of your Job Search Survival Toolkit.

33. Accomplishment Stories Are Your Most Powerful Selling Tools

What is an accomplishment story? It's one or more of the following:

- A work-related task or event about which you feel proud
- A situation where you exceeded the job's responsibilities
- A specific instance of your taking personal initiative
- A time when you may have received special recognition or praise

Select five or six work-related events from any time in your career, and answer the following five questions to complete your accomplishment stories. Each of your answers should constitute its own paragraph on the page (so each story consists of five paragraphs). The stories should be written on separate pages (one story per sheet), following the five-step structure shown as follows. Give a short title to each story, and type it at the top of each respective page.

1. What was the problem, need, or challenge?
2. What did you do about it? (Not the team or department—*you*)
3. How did you do it, specifically?
4. What positive, tangible results did you produce? (Quantify if possible)
5. What skills did you demonstrate?* (List three to four skill words for each story.)

*Skill words include the following. Use only these words, selecting three to four maximum per story, to answer question 5: *management, observation, communication, leadership, presentation, persuasion, analysis, innovation, team-building, problem-solving, follow-through, organization*.

Here's a list to help jog your memory about your own career accomplishments:

Have you ever...

- Managed teams, departments, or projects?
- Saved money for your department or company?
- Achieved greater results with limited/fewer resources?
- Received special recognition, awards, or letters of commendation?
- Implemented new systems, processes, or procedures?
- Opened new client accounts or expanded an existing one?
- Increased your company's productivity or profitability?
- Solved an unusually challenging business problem?
- Increased sales revenue?
- Been promoted or given more responsibility?

- Achieved something that had never been done before at your company?
- Designed or developed something unique?
- Written papers or reports, or conducted presentations?
- Trained or mentored employees?
- Increased efficiency or speed?
- Recognized challenges before they became real problems?
- Improved safety standards?
- Brought in projects under budget and before deadline?
- Exceeded expectations of the boss?
- Organized and carried out new initiatives?

Tips:

1. Use strong action verbs at the beginning of every sentence. Avoid passive-sounding phrases, such as "responsible for."
2. Quantify your results whenever possible, demonstrating tangible, measurable outcomes.

Example: Accomplishment Story (Downloadable)

Managing Marketing Communications and Saving $250K

What was the problem or need?
In the mid-1990s, Boyd Contract Services needed a strong, updated marketing communications and public relations program. Many collateral pieces were terribly out-of-date, and there was no real, organized public relations (PR) effort. The quarterly customer newsletter was perpetually late and had no consistent editorial slant or storyboard. The division truly needed an agency that would be attentive to its needs and would partner with it, at a reasonable cost.

(*Continued*)

What did you do about it?

I was asked to manage the marketing communications/PR function, in addition to my other responsibilities (forecasting, strategic planning, market research). I agreed to do this, with the understanding that I would have the authority to make decisions and recommendations.

How did you do it, specifically?

I contacted several local Boston-area agencies, especially looking at those who had experience with industrial companies such as ours. I also contacted the company's in-house Creative Services department and asked them to put together a proposal. I canvassed our regional sales managers and marketing managers to understand what their marketing communications needs and priorities were. I found that in several instances, frustration with the poor service from the New York agency had led some regional offices and managers to use regional agencies or local artists and freelancers—another example of how the division as a whole was not spending its PR money efficiently. Finally, following my interviews with the agencies, I presented to the VP of Sales & Marketing my recommendation: go with the in-house company agency.

What positive, tangible results did you produce? (Quantify if possible)

The quality of the newsletter improved tremendously, and we also began to get regular press coverage, due to the communications plan Creative Services put together for us. However, the strongest outcome of moving these communications activities in-house was the savings of a quarter-million dollars ($250,000) in the first year alone.

What skills did you demonstrate? (include three or four maximum)

Leadership, analysis, persuasion, follow-through

To download this element of your Job Search Survival Toolkit, visit: www.CareerPotential.com/bookbonus.

34. Verbal Presentations: What to Say and How to Say It

The next two tools in the Job Search Survival Toolkit are very important: your Positioning Statement and Departure Statement. Preparing these in advance, and memorizing them, will keep you from getting into trouble at the interview. Just as an actor would not dream of going out on stage before learning her lines, you should not begin your job search until you're prepared and memorized your verbal statements. Once you've written and incorporated these statements, your confidence will improve dramatically—and so will your results.

Here's What You'll Need:

1. Prepare and practice a Positioning Statement (also known as a 30-second commercial) about who you are professionally, the industries you've served, and the particular strengths you can contribute to a new employer.
2. You'll also need a prepared statement that explains why and how you departed from your previous employer, or why you're seeking a new position (even if you're still working). This verbal presentation is called your Departure Statement.

Tips:

1. When you write out these verbal tools, keep them brief and then memorize them so they will always be on the tip of your tongue.
2. Both of these statements can and should be used in any and all situations—with friends, colleagues, networking partners, on job interviews, and later in the search process. Here are a few examples:

Example: Positioning Statement #1

My background is in Project Management. I have 10 years of experience in the human resources field, and my work has focused mostly on executive search. In this role, I have contributed my skills in organization, problem solving, management, and communication. I am most proud of my track record of improving efficiency, enhancing productivity, and developing profitable business processes. I am seeking an opportunity where I can make a positive impact on the bottom line and empower people to achieve operational excellence.

Example: Departure Statement #1

Digital Ventures has been a wonderful place to work and build my skills, and I have made a positive impact on the company. However, at this point, I believe that the time is right to explore new opportunities. I am looking forward to using my proven organizational, problem-solving, and management skills to make a significant contribution to another organization.

Example: Positioning Statement #2

I am a senior accomplished sales and marketing professional with more than 20 years of increasing responsibility in the document and information-handling marketplace. My strengths include leadership, problem solving, analysis, and persuasion. In my sales career, I have exceeded goals 15 out of 20 eligible years. I have worked effectively with third-party partners and brokers, and have conducted direct sales to many Fortune 500 companies.

Example: Departure Statement #2

As a result of declining market conditions, Konix has undergone a major reorganization. This has resulted in the elimination of more than 200 positions from the national sales force, including mine. I am now exploring leadership opportunities that will take full advantage of my 20 years of outstanding technology sales experience.

Guidelines for Your Positioning Statement

Your Positioning Statement must:

- State succinctly what your professional identity is (e.g., Quality Assurance Manager) and level (e.g., entry level or senior)
- Convey approximately how many years of experience you have
- Highlight industries or functions in which you have expertise

- List specific strengths (e.g, problem solving, team building, leadership, etc.)
- Indicate what you're looking for in a new position

Exercise: Positioning Statement (Downloadable)

Use the following template to jump-start your writing, and then feel free to rewrite and fine-tune until you have something that works well.

My background is in (provide professional "tag" or identifier) ____

____

____

I have __________ years of experience in the __________ industry, and my work has focused on ______________________________

____

____

____

____

____

____

My specific roles and functions have included ______________

____

____

____

I am most proud of ____

____

____

____

____

____

____

(*Continued*)

I am now seeking an opportunity (describe the type of position or role you are seeking—not the title—as precisely as you can, along with what/how you can contribute) ______________________________
____
____
____
____

To download this element of your Job Search Survival Toolkit, visit: www.CareerPotential.com/bookbonus.

Guidelines for Your Departure Statement

Your Departure Statement must:

- Be positive in tone
- Take the focus off you, and put your departure into a larger context (e.g., "they had a layoff of 500 people" or "company was acquired," etc.)
- Demonstrate that you carry no emotional baggage about what happened
- Show that you have a clear idea of where you're headed professionally

Exercise: Departure Statement (Downloadable)

Use the following template to jump-start your writing, and then feel free to rewrite and fine-tune until you have something that works well.

Provide a time frame (i.e., in 2009; for the past 5 years; 2 months ago . . .)
____
____

(Company Name) experienced (layoff, consolidation, change of management, new strategy, different priorities)

____

____

____

As a result, ____________ positions were affected, including mine.

____

____

____

____

I'm now exploring opportunities (that will take advantage of my/that will leverage my/where I will be able to contribute . . .)

____

____

To download this element of your Job Search Survival Toolkit, visit: www.CareerPotential.com/bookbonus.

35. Your Professional Biography Will Be Your Most Frequently Used Tool

A lot of job seekers make the mistake of giving everyone they meet a copy of their resume. That is *not* the proper use of your resume. As we said earlier, your resume should be one of the *least* frequently used tools in your Job Search Survival Toolkit. Your Professional Biography (bio) should act as your calling card.

> Because more than 80 percent of your job search efforts will be in networking, the Professional Biography will be your most frequently used tool.

Because more than 80 percent of your job search efforts will be in networking, the bio will be your *most* frequently used tool. The bio is simply a one-page narrative of your career, written in paragraph form, in the third person—as though someone else wrote it about you. This is certainly no time to be shy, so make it sound impressive. The bio really speaks to your reputation and character, much more than a resume does. The interesting thing about Professional Biographies is how few working professionals know about them—much less use them to full advantage.

Think about it: even if you're not in a job search, your bio should always be up-to-date and current. Why? Because you'll need it...

- If you're applying for a project internally
- If you're presenting your firm's credentials to a potential client
- If you're asked to speak at an industry conference or trade association meeting
- If you're responding to a journalist to be quoted in the media
- If you write an article for publication
- If you want to present a professional image to the world without ever hinting at the fact that you may be looking for other opportunities

Read over the examples on the following pages to get the feel of what a good bio looks like. Later, we'll put yours together, paragraph by paragraph, and you'll have a chance to polish it into its final format.

36. Developing a Target Company List Builds Your Momentum and Focus

Now that you've detailed the *kinds* of companies you're after, it's time to identify the *names* of those companies. Refer back to your Employer Wish List. Then, select broad industry categories where your skills, experiences, and interests would be a good fit. Examples would be Healthcare or Professional Services or Consumer Products.

Begin to research specific organizations that meet your criteria in each of those industries. You'll gather as much information on them as you can and network your way in to meet with the hiring managers (not Human Resources) at these companies. The sooner you target specific employers, the sooner you'll get to meet with them (yes, even if they claim they're not hiring.)

The sooner you target specific employers, the sooner you'll get to meet with them (yes, even if they claim they're not hiring.)

Sample: Professional Biography #1

Joan Manuto

555 Davids Drive
Moylan, VA 19322

Cell: 555-655-5555
jmanuto@cp.com

Joan Manuto is a **Senior Operating Executive** with over twenty years of experience in improving corporate performance and value. Her positions have been with Fortune 100 companies in the financial services and telecommunications fields. Ms. Manuto has a successful track record of improving profits by increasing sales, developing products and markets, and managing significant cost containment over the last five years at GBR Capital Corp. She has had both P&L accountability and operating accountability in the insurance industry and the consulting field. Ms. Manuto is accomplished in quality tools and methodology, having used business process redesign and process management successfully at both Krascorp and GBR to drive significant top-line and bottom-line improvements.

Ms. Manuto has had a varied career that includes sales, operations, investor relations, and consulting. She has built operations and organizations in remittance processing, quality consulting, and insurance. Ms. Manuto is a results-oriented professional who has consistently demonstrated expertise in visualizing strategic direction and moving organizations through the change management necessary to achieve desired objectives. She has successfully created two quality operations and managed several acquisition integrations.

Representative accomplishments include:

- Increased sales and aggressively managed costs in multiple businesses through use of quality methodology. At GBR, outsourced administrative function, resulting in $3 million annual savings. Identified and executed sales projects, resulting in $2.5 million in net income, and reengineered the sourcing and billing processes for an additional $1 million.
- Served as integration leader at GBR for two acquisitions, resulting in reduced staff and associated expenses by 50% while growing sales 10%.
- Developed and executed GBR Six Sigma Quality programs and initiatives, credited with contributing $5+ million in net income, while controlling budgets to 20% below target.
- Improved customer satisfaction rating by 8% and reduced employee turnover by 12% through restructuring, and reengineered business processes for five Krascorp Call Centers with 5,000+ employees.

Ms. Manuto holds an M.B.A. from Purdue University, and an undergraduate degree from University of Minnesota with a concentration in Finance. She has participated in significant quality training from both Krascorp and GBR, and is a certified Six Sigma Master Black Belt.

Ms. Manuto is actively involved in her church's youth groups and parents' associations at her children's middle and elementary schools. She has traveled extensively for both business and pleasure.

Sample: Professional Biography #2

Frederick Mercury

566 Laurel Lane
Newbury, NY 18008

Cell: 555-337-8888
Home: 555-777-9999

fkm6h4566@yahoo.net

Fred Mercury is a **Senior Sales and Marketing Executive** with more than 20 years' experience driving profitable revenue and market share growth in top Fortune 50 companies. Most recently, Fred was the President of the Philadelphia Marketplace for XCS, a world leader in the document management and services industry. His strategic expertise, field sales leadership, and ability to embrace change to capture new opportunities enabled XCS Philadelphia to achieve the #1 position in the Mid-Atlantic District. Operating Income was at 105% with $14.2 million total revenue and 12% year-over-year growth in customer satisfaction and employee retention.

Prior to XCS, Fred was the head of Medicare Sales and Marketing for Alixa Healthcare, the industry leader in managed care. His general management expertise, action orientation, and customer relationship management skills enabled Alixa to achieve record growth of over $4 billion in Medicare sales and 700,000 members.

Before joining Alixa, Fred spent the majority of his career at Beebop Corporation, where he directed numerous sales and customer operations. Fred has a reputation as a results-oriented manager who embraces change and utilizes total quality management principles in conjunction with employee empowerment to achieve outstanding results.

While Fred's primary area of expertise is sales and marketing, he brings a General Manager's perspective to running a business and achieving balanced results across all critical performance criteria. Representative accomplishments include:

- Integrated the four primary XCS business while merging two marketplaces and still achieved the distinction as the #1 performing marketplace in the Mid-Atlantic District for the XCS common goals of business results, customer satisfaction, and employee satisfaction.
- Played a key role in corporate strategic planning initiative commissioned by the President of Alixa, to identify future strategic direction and vital priorities.
- Developed and implemented a strategic plan for Beebop indirect channels expansion, including Office Supplies Superstores, Agents, Dealers, and Catalogue Sales. Grew revenue in excess of 30% annually and achieved double-digit growth in all four indirect channels.
- Implemented customer relationship management partnership with the outside supplies sales organization, while running the Beebop Supplies Telesales Centers nationally. Enabled Beebop Supplies to achieve 10% growth in revenue and 14% in profits.

Fred graduated from New York University with a B.A. in Economics. He then attended Stanford University School of Business in the evening and received an M.B.A. while starting a family and working full-time as a Sales Manager for Beebop.

Fred lives in Newbury, NY, with his wife and two children. He leads an active lifestyle, participating in many sporting activities, such as skiing, baseball, football, and basketball. Fred is dedicated to physical fitness and enjoys working around the house.

Exercise: Professional Biography (Downloadable)

_________________________ is a _________________________
with extensive experience in
____

Most recently, _______________________________________
____

His/Her specific areas of expertise are:______________________
____

In addition,____
____

Career highlights include: ______________________________
____

Some areas of significant accomplishment include:

- ____
- ____
- ____
- ____
- ____

Throughout his/her career, ____________ has always been known for____
____
____

He/She has. ____
____

With major interests in __________, ___________, __________,
___________ enjoys all aspects of his/her lifestyle. ___________
graduated from ___________________ ___________________
with (academic highlights).

To download this element of your Job Search Survival Toolkit, visit: www.CareerPotential.com/bookbonus.

Your main goal is to systematically go after each company on your list (through networking) and meet with the hiring managers at those firms. Don't get distracted or sidetracked by other companies or easy-ins at companies that are *not* on your list. When the job market is tight and the headlines are screaming about dire economic conditions, it may be emotionally challenging to focus exclusively on your target list, but that's exactly how successful people get a job when no one's hiring. You'll then interview the representatives of these companies, and determine which organization you would like to hire as your new employer.

Here are Some Sources to Begin Researching Your Target Companies:

- Friends, family, colleagues, neighbors who might know the inside scoop at some of your target companies
- Networking to find current or past employees at your target companies, and hearing what the organization is like firsthand
- *Fortune Magazine*'s list of 100 Great Places to Work in America, or www.greatplacetowork.com
- Business articles in your local daily newspaper's business section
- Your local edition of American City Business Journals' "Book of Lists" (www.bizjournals.com)
- Social networking media web sites that connect professionals, such as LinkedIn (www.linkedin.com)
- Your local Chambers of Commerce and trade associations, or industry organizations that your target companies may be a member of
- Target companies' web sites and downloadable annual reports
- Use Google (www.google.com) to do a search on the company or its top executives, and see what kinds of articles and stories come up
- Fee-based databases that you may access for free at your local public library, including *Hoover's* and *Dun & Bradstreet's Million Dollar Database*
- Other web resources, such as www.vault.com

By the time you're finished, you should be able to generate a very specific list of 35 to 50 target organizations, like the sample outline

Sample: Target Company List (Downloadable)

JENNIFER KINSEY

1443 Fernam Drive
Monroe, MA 55225
Cell: 555-444-3333
E-mail: jk2929@eastmail.net

Finance/Insurance
SEI Investments
ACE/INA
Advanta
MBNA
Delaware Investments
ING Direct
CIGNA Commerce Bank
PNC Bank
Vanguard Group
Penn Mutual Life Insurance
Mellon PSFS
Merrill Lynch
Morgan Stanley
State Farm

Consulting/Professional Services
Ernst and Young
Accenture
Deloitte
PwC Consulting
EDS
Towers Perrin
Boston Consulting Group
Unconsulting
Aon Consulting
Booz Allen Hamilton

Comm./Advertising
DirecTV
Netplus Marketing
Dorland Health Comm.
Archer Xavier
HBO
Xpress Communications
TV Guide
WHYY
WNBC
WNET

Higher Education
University of Pennsylvania
The Wharton School
Drexel University
Villanova University
Bryn Mawr College
Stanford Business School

Technology
SAP
Microsoft
Sun Microsystems
Hewlett Packard
IBM

Pharma/Healthcare
Merck
AstraZeneca
Johnson & Johnson
Aventis
Independence Blue Cross
Jefferson Health System
Glaxo SmithKline
ViroPharma
Wyeth
Amerisource Bergen
Neose Technologies
Orthovita

Other
Sunoco
Ikon
Siemens
Verizon Wireless
Subaru
PepsiCo
WL Gore
Du Pont

To download this element of your Job Search Survival Toolkit, visit: www.CareerPotential.com/bookbonus.

seen on page 71. Remember, these are the companies that seem to match the criteria you already developed in your Company Wish List.

37. Deploy an Army of People Who Can Help You: Build Your Contact List

Your Contact List is a comprehensive list of people who meet *one and only one criteria*: if they were asked the question, "Do you know who (your name) is?" they would answer "Yes." The *only* reason anyone should *not* be on your Contact List is if you know for a fact that they do not like you.

Compile a list of all (yes, *all*) of the people you know personally and professionally. Most clients create a database file of these people in a popular software program such as Microsoft Outlook or Excel. Is this going to be a large list? You bet it is. Probably more than 200 people strong. Some of my clients come in with lists as large as 400 or 500 names! Should you really have all of these names on your list? Yes, you should, especially if you're serious about landing the best possible job in the worst possible job market.

Create three columns on your document, for your contacts' names, phone numbers, and e-mail addresses. Don't edit the list or make any assumptions about who can or can't help you. You might be surprised! List *everyone*—including your tailor, your mail carrier, your dentist, your neighbors—as well as everyone with whom you have worked (colleagues, customers, vendors, suppliers, and industry contacts). These people can and should be from every level—secretaries, cafeteria workers, presidents, CEOs, salespeople, middle managers, janitors, and finance specialists. Remember that approximately 80 percent of new opportunities are secured through networking, and a very high percentage of those positions are discovered through people who were *least* expected to be of help.

Approximately 80 percent of new opportunities are secured through networking, and a very high percentage of those positions are discovered through people who were least expected to be of help.

38. Professional References Help You Prove You're the Real Deal

The recommended number of phone reference people is between four and six, and you should secure at least three to four solid letters of recommendation. Most people already know that they need a list of professional references. But you might be asking, "Why do I need letters of recommendation at this point in my career?" The answer is simple: When you find yourself in a competitive interviewing situation (and what interviewing situation is *not* competitive?), letters of recommendation can really help push you over the top. In other words, when two or more candidates are equally qualified, the one who provides strong letters of recommendation at the later stages of the interview process will get the offer. So why not have this extra ammunition in your arsenal?

Here's How to Create Your List of Professional References and Generate Your Letters of Recommendation:

1. Make a list of all the people you know who would vouch for you and lend support in your job search. (These must be people who know you professionally, *not* friends and relatives.)
2. Separate them into two categories—one group to write letters of recommendation and the other to appear on your list of professional references.
3. Call and ask them all for their help, stating exactly what you want them to do, and soliciting their participation.
4. Send them each a packet, including these four items: Cover Letter, Professional Biography, Resume, and Target Company List (your cover letter includes a bullet list of the specific attributes or experiences you want them to focus on in their letter or phone call). It's a good idea to send an e-mail with attachments, and also hardcopies via U.S. mail. *Note*: the cover letter you send to the letter writers will be slightly different from the letter you send to the phone reference people.
5. Follow up to be sure they received everything and that they fully understand your documents.
6. Tell the phone reference people to inform you immediately when they receive any calls from target companies. (Knowing this will be very valuable to you.)

7. Tell the letter writers that you want to review their rough drafts and check them for accuracy. You'll have the chance to make minor edits and corrections. Give them a specific date by which they must send you their first drafts.
8. Offer to help each of these participants in a similar capacity, should the need ever arise.

> When you find yourself in a competitive interviewing situation, letters of recommendation can really help to push you over the top.

39. Letters of Recommendation Demonstrate Your Bottom-Line Value

Provide These General Tips to Your Letter Writers:

- Print the final letter on your company letterhead. If your employer does not permit you to write such letters on company letterhead, then please use your personal letterhead or create a simple letterhead (name, address, phone, e-mail at top of the sheet).
- Do not date the letter, do not include any salutation (there should be no "Dear ______"), and do not write "To Whom it May Concern" nor "Dear Sir/Madam."
- Keep the letter fairly brief, and never more than one page.

Letter Outline with Examples

Here is some additional direction you can give to the people who will be writing your letters of recommendation (adapt to your own situation and background):

The first paragraph should say something like:

"I am writing to you on behalf of my former colleague, Sally M. Smith. I had the privilege of working with her from (use dates) when she was the (title) of (company XYZ)." ***Use your own words.***

In the second paragraph, mention some specifics that you recall about me:

"As the (title/company), Sally directed the strategic planning process for our division and led the economic and market forecasting.

Her forecasts were instrumental in several projects, including A, B, and C. She actively contributed to the composites industry by doing (D, E, and F). Sally consistently demonstrated (words such as *leadership, problem solving, communication, follow-through, analysis,* and *organization* are good to use). Throughout her tenure with company XYZ, she proved herself to be _______ and a _______." (Or something along those lines. Focus your attention on my contributions to the company as much as possible.) ***Again, use your own words.***

For paragraph 3, you may wish to mention some personal traits/values of mine:

What was it like to work with me, how did I measure up as a team member compared with others? What contributions was I known for? What was I particularly good at? What positive recollections of working with me do you have? ***Use whatever adjectives come to mind.***

The last paragraph should reiterate how you feel about me as a professional:

"I feel strongly that Sally would bring _______, _______, and _______ to any organization and prove to be a valuable, contributing member" (or something similar). End with a sentence that says something like, "I would be happy to talk with you if you have any questions about Sally," or "Please feel free to contact me directly if you would like to know more about her work." ***Use your own words***.

Telephone References: Whom to Ask and How to Ask

You'll also need a list of professional references. Make a list of colleagues who sincerely respect and admire your work. Again, these should be people who know you professionally (from any time in your career), *not* friends and relatives.

Contact each of them, and get approval to use their names on your list of professional references. Be sure to provide these individuals with specific guidance about what to say when prospective employers call. Also, ask these references to contact you immediately if any prospective employers call them. On page 79, you'll find an example of a list of professional references. Create your own list. Be sure to include a statement after each reference indicating what their relationship to you is. Also, always use the prefixes Mr., Ms., or Dr., as appropriate, before each name.

Sample: Request for a Letter of Recommendation

Date

Dear ______:

Thank you for speaking with me yesterday regarding my career search and networking activities. I appreciate your willingness to assist me.

In order to make the process as easy for you as possible, I have enclosed three documents to give you an overview of my professional background. These include my: Resume, Professional Biography, and Target Company List.

Please prepare a rough draft of your recommendation letter and send it to me by ______________. I will check the document for accuracy and return it promptly with any necessary changes. The final letter should be printed on your company letterhead and signed by you.

Thank you again for your assistance. I would be happy to help you in a similar capacity, should the need ever arise.

Cordially,

Your name here

Enclosures/Attachments

Sample: Letter of Recommendation

John Gergen

150 Lapham Lane
Chesterfield, PA 19425
ager265ts41@msn.net
(555) 555-8888

I have had the pleasure of knowing and working with Allan Stevens for almost 13 years.

I first met Allan at Midland Mutual Life in 1993, when I was brought in to become head of marketing and operations. It was immediately apparent to me that Allan was a driving force within Midland, having been the impetus behind Midland's best-selling term plans, and I made him a General Manager of one of the SBUs we set up. Allan excelled in that role, implementing product changes and turning around a losing operation.

I then promoted him into a new role as head of Product Research and Development. Again, Allan rose to the occasion, enhancing the term and UL lines and developing our BioEdge product, which was the first product in the industry to use multiple underwriting classes.

When I joined CNA as president of the life company, I recruited Allan to come with me. As Vice President of Special Operations, he directed mergers and acquisitions, variable products, and Canadian life operations, impressively building a major presence in the Canadian life market in a short time. Later, while consulting for Coventry, I had the opportunity to see Allan play a critical role in analyzing and negotiating structured finance arrangements for a new asset class for Coventry, eventually obtaining over $100 million of financing.

Allan is without question one of the brightest and most effective people I have met in my career. His creativity and leadership really helped me in my roles, and his analytic and problem-solving skills are particularly strong. He has excellent relationships with reinsurers and field personnel. Allan has become a good and loyal friend and a talented executive, and I would highly recommend him to your firm.

Sincerely,

John Gergen

Sample: Request for a Telephone Reference

Dear Ms. Fromm:

Thank you for agreeing to be one of my professional phone references!

I would like to make this process as easy for you as possible. Therefore, I have enclosed several documents that describe my professional background and goals. This information will provide talking points for you to use during conversations with anyone who calls you inquiring about me. If you have any questions about this material, just let me know.

When you are contacted by any prospective employer, I would appreciate it if you would let me know right away. You can email me at joetmiller@catandmouse.net or call me at 555-555-9939. I would be happy to assist you in a similar capacity, should the need ever arise. Thank you again for your time and consideration.

Sincerely,

Joseph R. Miller

Enclosures/Attachments

Sample: Professional References (Downloadable)

James E. Bresser

700672 Bloomfield Avenue
Montclair, NJ 07042

555-555-7777 (Cell)
555-555-5555 (Home)
bresserjr@aol.com

Mr. Don Loy, Senior Accountant
Ibsen Office Solutions, Inc.
555 Windy Way
Merion, PA 19050
Telephone: 555-555-7109
E-mail: dloy@ibsensol.com

Don and I have been business associates for the last six years. I met Don while a member of the Aiken Healthcare Senior Management Team.

Mr. Michael Kardonsky, Former President
Aiken Healthcare
777 Bloomfield Avenue, Suite 200
Bedford, PA 18905
Telephone: 555-555-3143
E-mail: mkardonsky1@comcast.com

Mike gave me my first full-time job as a Sales Trainee at Jedford Machines. He also hired me at Aiken Healthcare and I reported to him. I have known Mike for over 20 years.

Mr. Thomas Dugans, Corporate Senior Vice President
Jedford Machines
222 Bowling Green Avenue
Rockland, NY 12501
Telephone: 555-555-2652
E-mail: thomas.j.dugans@jedfordmachines.com

Tom and I worked together as peers for many years, and he progressed to senior management positions prior to becoming President at Gardenia Group.

Mr. William Smith, Mid Atlantic Sales Manager
Ibsen Office Solutions, Inc.
555 Windy Way
Merion, PA 19050
Telephone: 555-555-3405
E-mail: bsmith@ibsensol.com

I reported directly to Bill in my capacity as Philadelphia Sales Representative.

Mr. Ken Millard, President
Imperon Associates
5067 Coast Highway
Albany, CA 90210
Telephone: 555-555-5570
E-mail: imperonken@aol.com

I met Ken 20 years ago while at Jedford Machines, and have maintained a business and personal relationship since then.

To download this element of your Job Search Survival Toolkit, visit: www.CareerPotential.com/bookbonus.

PART IV

Job Search Tactics to Use When No One's Hiring

40. Networking Is Not *Part* of Your Job Search—Networking *Is* Your Job Search

You're now ready to begin networking with people who can help you reach the hiring managers inside your target companies. Networking can be done over the phone, in person, via e-mail, or even over a cup of coffee or lunch. The main thing to remember is that, in general, people *want* to help others.

Networking makes most people feel good about themselves. It boosts their self-esteem to connect people with opportunities—especially when those opportunities are hard to come by—and it makes them feel important. The bottom line is that these people really *are* quite important to your career success. (Just as *you* may have been very important to the career success of others in the past—and certainly will be again in the future.)

> The main thing to remember is that, in general, people want to help others.

No matter what the unemployment headlines say, don't ever let up on your networking efforts. More than 80 percent of my clients land great jobs through their networks. So, it's not worth risking those odds to *not* be continually networking during good economic times and bad, whether you love your job or you're out of work.

Networking should be the primary focus of everything you do. The quantity and quality of your networking time is directly related to the personal, professional, and financial satisfaction you'll have in your current job or your next job, and for the rest of your professional life.

Just in case you're a little intimidated about the notion of networking (and again, you *shouldn't* be), let's review for a moment some of the reasons why someone would actually *want* to have a networking conversation with you:

1. They might (secretly) be looking for a job soon themselves, and they can learn from your approach.
2. They might gain new information about their industry or their competition—plus other knowledge or perspective that you bring.
3. They like to feel important, have their ego stroked, and feel that their advice is valued and respected.
4. Many people genuinely want to help, and they find it gratifying to be of service.
5. They might be bored, and you can provide welcome relief from their normal routine.
6. They're happy to do a favor for the person who referred you, by agreeing to network with you.
7. They've been through a job search or career transition themselves, so they empathize with you.

When it's done properly, networking is not about taking, but rather about giving. You must always come from an attitude of generosity during the networking process. After every networking conversation, the other person should feel genuinely glad that you contacted them and feel enriched by the experience. Now that you're convinced that networking is truly a win–win proposition (and it is!), here are some tools and strategies to get you going.

41. Great Networkers Are *Not* Great Talkers; They're Great Listeners

Networking is a lot simpler (and less scary) than many people think. You do not need to be a great schmoozer to network effectively. The best networkers are often great *listeners*, more than great *talkers*.

Here are the basic steps of the networking process:

1. Use your Contact List to focus on specific people to reach out to each week.
2. Use the Networking Meeting Agenda below and develop your own version of a Networking Script (also described below.)
3. Meet people in neutral locations if possible—over coffee, lunch, or breakfast.
4. Leverage the notion of six degrees of separation—ask for contacts from your contacts, and you can connect with almost anyone.
5. Reach out by e-mail, phone, or letter.
6. The formula goes: Meet, Ask, Listen, Learn, Act, Thank.
7. Follow up after your meeting and keep the conversation going with a two-way value exchange. Don't love 'em and leave 'em. Grow your stay-in-touch network. Use the mini-newsletter format I'll share with you to make this easy and consistent.

> Remember: If you're in career transition, networking *is* your job.

You should be spending at least 80 percent of your job search time networking—and about 20 percent of your time and effort on everything else.

If someone won't network with you, you must not take it personally. Adopt this mindset from the world of direct sales—"some will, some won't, so what, next!" Keep working your network, and don't let the occasional rejection deter you. It's a smart career move to *always be networking,* no matter what's going on for you professionally. If you don't need help at this time, build up your networking power by helping others. It will always pay big dividends in the long run.

42. Never "Wing it" When You're Networking—Use an Agenda

Here is a basic agenda to follow in an initial phone outreach (see Network Agenda #1). My main piece of advice to you for networking

Sample: Networking Agenda #1 (Downloadable)

Meeting Agenda		***Name***
Location	***Time***	***Date***
Meeting Objective: Document Review, Feedback/Advice, and Networking Contacts		

Please Read:	Professional Biography and Target Company List

	Participants
1.	
2.	

	Topics
1.	Meeting Purpose
2.	My Background
3.	Document Review and Feedback – My Professional Biography
4.	Document Review and Feedback – My Target Company List
5.	Specific Names/Leads You Can Give Me
6.	Other Opportunities/Possibilities I Should Consider
7.	Next Steps
8.	What Can I Do for You?

	Follow-Up Steps
1.	
2.	
3.	
4.	
5.	

	Networking Contact	**Organization**	**Phone Number**	**E-mail Address**
1.			( ) -	
2.			( ) -	
3.			( ) -	
4.			( ) -	
5.			( ) -	

To download this element of your Job Search Survival Toolkit, visit: www.CareerPotential.com/bookbonus.

success is: just be yourself. Don't try too hard during these networking meetings. Relax, and follow the agenda very closely.

Begin by asking, "Is this a good time for you to talk?" (If it isn't, identify a different time to call the person back.) Then move the conversation forward in this manner:

1. Build rapport
2. Update on where you have been (use Positioning Statement)
3. Explain what happened (use Departure Statement)
4. Ask for help (would you be willing to help me?)
5. Decompress by taking the pressure off (reassure them you are not asking for a job)
6. Ask again for help (expanding contact network/guidance/advice/feedback)
7. Thank them—set a time to get back to them

If you look at Network Agenda #1 and #2, you'll see some very practical forms that my clients have used with great success. Copy and use them, or adapt them to your own style.

Network Agenda #2 on the following page is an example of an agenda document that you can adapt, fill in, and actually hand to your networking partner as you sit down to start a meeting.

43. Meeting with Hiring Managers Is Your Number-One Speed Advantage

There is a direct correlation between how many hiring managers you meet with and how quickly you'll land a great job. This is true in any job market, and it's even more critical to your job search success when no one's hiring.

There is a direct correlation between how many hiring managers you meet with and how quickly you'll land a great job.

Sample: Networking Agenda #2 (Downloadable)

Name:

Date/Time:

---

1. Catch-up and introductions

2. Purpose of the meeting

3. Discussion of my situation

4. Review of Target Company List and Professional Biography

5. How you can help me

6. Ideas and contacts

7. How I can help you

8. Follow-up steps

To download this element of your Job Search Survival Toolkit, visit: www.CareerPotential.com/bookbonus.

The number of hiring managers you meet with is a good barometer of how effective *all* of your networking efforts are. No matter what, don't get discouraged and don't take it personally. Keep going after meetings with hiring managers and people who can get you in front of hiring managers.

As you proceed through your career transition, it will be important to track your performance day-to-day and week-to-week. This is how you'll gauge your productivity and effectiveness. The goal is obviously to continually improve your performance and produce better results. If you can't measure it, you can't manage it.

Networking Tips for a Tight Job Market

- Schedule face to face meetings with Centers of Influence (CoIs).
- Schedule phone meetings with other people who might lead you to CoIs.
- Get at least three to five names from each person with whom you speak.
- Keep the first phone conversation very brief (no more than five to seven minutes).
- Be confident and purposeful.
- Send your Target Company List and Professional Biography immediately after the first conversation.
- Bring a prepared list of questions and ask if it's okay to jot down notes as you talk.
- Establish good rapport by getting the other person to talk about himself or herself.
- If you ask for 20 minutes, keep the meeting to 20 minutes. Follow up shortly thereafter for feedback, contact names, information, and guidance.
- Ask if you may use your contact's name when calling people to whom they refer you.
- Don't use the words "job" or "fired".
- Don't make excuses or sound apologetic.
- Come from generosity (look for opportunities to offer something of value).
- *Always* send a thank-you note immediately after your meeting.

44. Masters of Networking Use a Networking Script

Please understand that career networking is different than what you may think it is. This is true for those of you with an outgoing personality who have done lots of networking in the past, and perhaps even more true for those who don't have an outgoing personality and have less networking experience.

Networking is not about being charming, or selling someone on the idea of hiring you. It's about purposefully and gracefully asking peers for help, advice, input, and contacts—and offering genuine value in return. And as I mentioned earlier, most people really do want to be helpful.

On the following page, you'll see an example of a Networking Script, which you should adapt to your own style and personality. When you're in a networking phone conversation or meeting, *don't read* the script, but *do* follow its structure and format very closely.

During this first meeting, you'll be presenting your Professional Biography and Target Company List—the two primary tools used for networking. Once the other person has reviewed these two documents, and has had time to think about the people you should meet, you'll have a follow-up appointment in order to get the specific help you need. Be sure to set the follow-up date and time before you end the first conversation, and make sure to enter it into your calendar so it will really happen.

> Your Professional Biography and Target Company List are the two primary tools used for networking.

45. When No One's Hiring, the Best Way to Get a Job Is *Not* to Look for a Job

In the course of your networking, the clearer you make it that you're *not* looking for a job at the present time, the more attractive you'll be to the hiring manager. This may seem counterintuitive, but it's true. The fact is that almost no one likes a job seeker, but nearly everyone likes a solutions provider.

> The fact is that almost no one likes a job seeker, but nearly everyone likes a solutions provider.

Sample: Networking Script (Downloadable)

Introduction

Hello ____________, my name is/this is______________. I was referred to you by ________________. I know ______ from ____________________. I'm contacting you about a career matter, but let me assure you that I am not calling to ask you for a job! Is this a good time for you? I only need 5-10 minutes of your time.

Build Rapport

I was referred by your (or "a mutual") colleague/friend, who suggested that....
(Find some area of common interest to discuss). Try to "connect" on a personal level.

Positioning Statement (Sample; paste your own Positioning Statement here)
I am a Senior Financial and Operations Professional and graduate of Western General's Financial Management Program. I have more than 15 years of experience in the Manufacturing and Services industries. My strengths include analysis, problem-solving, communication and innovation. I have specific expertise in Financial Analysis and Reporting, Cash and Risk Management, and Productivity Analysis. I am seeking a leadership position with a focus on Financial Reporting.

Departure Statement (Sample; paste your own Departure Statement here)
As a result of a merger between two business units, over 1,500 positions have been affected, including mine. I now have the opportunity to explore other career options in Financial Services that will leverage my proven strengths in analysis, problem-solving, communication and innovation.

Ask for help

Would you be willing to help me?

Decompress (take the pressure off)

Again, I am not asking you for a job, nor do I expect you to know of any appropriate openings. However, I am interested any advice or guidance that you could offer, in addition to any networking contacts you could provide. Would you be willing to review some of my credentials, and give me candid feedback? I could send the materials right over.

Wrap up

I will e-mail (or fax) a one-page *Professional Biography* and list of *Target Companies* to you. Then I'd like to follow-up and have another conversation – when would be better for you, Wednesday afternoon or Friday morning? I know your input will be of great value, and I appreciate your willingness to help.

To download this element of your Job Search Survival Toolkit, visit: www.CareerPotential.com/bookbonus.

The best outcome is when you add so much value to the conversation that it occurs to *the other person* to bring up the idea of working at their firm (or at another company they know of). That's called the no-selling sale, and it happens more often than you might expect.

46. Tracking Your Networking Is as Important as the Networking Itself

Just doing networking is a good start, but it's not enough. You need to organize, track, and follow up on every networking contact. Networking without follow-up is barely more effective than not networking. Someone who networks with 10 people and has an excellent follow-up and tracking system will do better than someone else who networks with 30 people and does no tracking or follow-up at all.

How can you make sure you'll do the follow-up and administrative work that's necessary to make a lasting impression? Schedule it! Yes, you read that right—put time aside in your calendar, day planner, or PDA for administrative and follow-up activities. When you have a one-on-one meeting or attend a networking event, make an appointment with yourself later that day or the next morning to write e-mails, make phone calls, and write thank-you notes. If you don't schedule it, it probably won't get done. You need to be organized, and you need to have a *system* to support you. Otherwise, all you'll be doing is meeting a lot of people and running around town for nothing.

You need to be organized, and you need to have a *system* to support you. Otherwise, all you'll be doing is meeting a lot of people and running around town for nothing.

Some people use a strategy of blocking out three specific times during the week for nothing but administrative work and follow-up calls. If you stay on top of it by making appointments with yourself, these vitally important follow-up tasks become easy, effortless, and even enjoyable. You'll feel good about being highly productive. Be sure to keep a detailed record of every call, letter, and meeting. Compare your results week to week, and keep improving your performance.

Please review the forms on the following pages, and use the one that's most appropriate for you. You can adapt your own versions based on these examples, and use them to track your own progress and keep an ongoing record of your meetings, conversations, and follow-ups. Make as many photocopies as you need, and keep these forms by your side to fill in as you conduct your networking calls and meetings.

Sample: Networking Tracking Form #1 (Downloadable)

Name:
Phone:
E-mail:
Source of Contact:

Notes/Background:

Date	Points of Discussion	Next Steps

To download this element of your Job Search Survival Toolkit, visit: www.CareerPotential.com/bookbonus.

Sample: Networking Tracking Form #2 (Downloadable)

Contact name:	Company name, address, and telephone:
Notes:	

To download this element of your Job Search Survival Toolkit, visit: www.CareerPotential.com/bookbonus.

47. The Networking Mini-Newsletter Helps You Stand Out When No One's Hiring

When you first start the networking process, you'll probably find it fairly easy to keep track of your meetings and stay in touch with your networking partners. But within a few weeks, and as your list grows, you'll learn that it gets much more challenging to keep in close touch with all of these people. A great way to follow up and keep in touch consistently with all of the people you meet—and to continue the value exchange that you started when you initially contacted them—is the mini-newsletter.

Sample: Mini-Newsletter

Dear Friends,

Welcome to the first edition of my mini-newsletter and networking journal. Since we have already been in contact regarding my career transition, I wanted to keep you informed of my progress and stay in touch with you! I'll be sending you an e-mail update like this every two to four weeks. If, for any reason, you would rather not hear from me is this format, please send me an e-mail now with the word "remove" in the subject line, and I'll delete your e-mail address from my list immediately.

NETWORKING

I have been fortunate to network or interview with some wonderful and generous people over the past few weeks! They include:

- The owners of a medium-sized facilities management company
- The Senior Vice President of Customer Care for a service organization
- A Placement Manager for a large staffing company
- A hiring manager for a major furniture and house wares retailer
- The owner of a large distribution center
- Human Resource managers for a manufacturing company
- A Divisional Manager for a nationwide travel and automotive services organization
- An Owner/Operator of a trucking firm
- A District Manager for a fortune 100 service organization
- A Vice President of Sales for a flooring company

I also attended the following networking events and career-related activities:
SHRM Career Management Forum: This is a subgroup of the HR professional organization that focuses on professional networking and career management. Information is available at www.phillyshrm.org.

I also attended a speech by Joe Paterno, the coach of Penn State's football team. I found it to be very inspirational. If you ever get a chance to hear Joe speak, go!

HOW YOU CAN HELP ME

I'm always looking for any thoughts, suggestions, or contacts you might have that can help me in my career transition and job search. One of the companies in the area that I would most like to get a contact with is Zip Industries. If you know anybody who works for the company, or who might have valuable information to share, I would appreciate you letting me know!

HOW CAN I HELP YOU?

During this transition period, I have come across many career search web sites, talked with several executive recruiters, and have had conversations with numerous hiring managers. Please let me know what I can do for you, from putting you in contact with someone to providing advice on professional networking. Give me a call or send me an e-mail anytime if I can ever be of help to you.

FINAL THOUGHTS

Thank you for your help and support during this transition process. Everyone I have contacted has been so eager to help! I really appreciate the time everybody has taken out of his or her busy schedule to assist me, and I sincerely hope to be of service to each of you at some point in the future!

I'll be back in touch with you in several weeks.

Mike Starr
Phone: 555-444-9999
E-mail: mstarr@corpcomco.net

When you think about business owners, salespeople, consultants, and freelancers, the concept of a newsletter or "e-zine" as a self-marketing tool seems obvious. Do you need to create an expensive, glossy newsletter like a big company might produce? Of course not! The easiest and most convenient way to deliver this information value exchange is via a simple e-mail format.

Instead of needing to repeatedly call everyone with whom you've networked, or write to them all individually, the mini-newsletter allows you to keep in touch and stay top-of-mind simply by hitting your computer's send button. Your mini-newsletter should be sent out to your contact list every two to four weeks, depending on your particular situation. Obviously, you should adapt the form, content, and tone to suit your own personality, as well as your industry, geography, and interests.

48. The Number-One Way to Get Hired When No One's Hiring

Once in a while, when your networking efforts have led to a meeting where you and the hiring manager truly click, the idea will occur to him or her to ask if you'd be interested in coming to work for their company. At that point, there may not even be a specific job opening at that company, but you've piqued the interviewer's interest enough to start the hiring conversation.

In this case, you should think about preparing a Work Proposal. This is a document in which you itemize your qualifications, skills, and accomplishments, and show how they align directly to the challenges, problems, and needs that the hiring manager has discussed with you. The Work Proposal is usually a one- or two-page document that outlines all of the different things you could do for the company and how you would generate results for them, based on the specific needs you uncovered during the networking meeting.

Because the Work Proposal usually grows out of a networking meeting, the letter takes a soft-sell approach. Rather than pushing for another meeting (as you would with other sorts of follow-up letters), you'll leave it in their hands. If the individual calls or writes you back, you'll know you've got something. The company may even create a position for you. If you don't get a response to the Work Proposal, this indicates that the company wasn't interested enough in you to engage in an ongoing dialogue. A sample Work Proposal appears next.

Sample: Work Proposal

March 7, 2009

Mr. Howard P. Sloane
President
Ibsen Consulting Group, Inc.
29 Rawlins Place
Barnesboro, PA 19374

Dear Mr. Sloane:

Thank you for meeting with me last week to discuss my current career activities and Ibsen Consulting Group, Inc. I was happy to learn more about the professional services your company offers, delivered by skilled, professional staff. Our talk about Ibsen helped me to better understand your business needs and challenges.

As you know, I took extensive notes during our meeting. As a result of our discussion, I have identified three major challenges that seem to be facing Ibsen Consulting Group, Inc. at this time. Coincidentally, these are areas in which I have specific expertise and a track record of significant accomplishment.

Mr. Sloane, you were very generous in sharing your time with me, and I would like to offer something of value in return. With this in mind, I have taken the liberty of outlining your company's apparent challenges below, along with some suggestions that may be helpful:

Your Challenges	Suggested Solutions
Revenue Growth/Business Development	• Create an independent Human Resource consulting practice with multiple service offerings.
Attract new members, expand product/service offerings, and build key client relationships	• Establish new projects and strengthen long-term relationships with major clients in a variety of industries. • Generate positive national press for high-profile projects, creating additional new business opportunities.
Leadership and People Management	• Recruit, hire, and direct an enthusiastic, motivated team to achieve higher customer ratings.
Coach, mentor, motivate, and lead by example, while measuring performance	• Coach executives to enhance their leadership skills. • Mentor high-potential employees by providing advice, instruction, observation, and feedback. • Establish employee performance goals, measurements, and rewards designed to collectively achieve organizational goals and encourage teamwork and team leadership.
Business and Financial Management	• Quickly achieve profitability in consulting practice.
Develop and control budgets, and manage service lines to maximize profitability	• Reduce salary costs by implementing a new staffing model. • Analyze volume and demand (including impact of pricing and marketing) and cost structures for service lines to design plans to maximize revenue growth and profitability.

I am confident that if you implement the measures I have suggested in this chart, you will begin to see the kind of results you spoke about at our meeting. If you would like to discuss my suggestions in greater detail, please feel free to contact me. I would be pleased to speak with you any time about these proven strategies.

Thank you again for giving me a more complete picture of Ibsen Consulting Group, Inc. I appreciate your time and interest.

Best Regards,

Jennifer Zolot

49. Create Your Online Career Identity—Blogs, Personal Web Site, and Social Media

In addition to the mini-newsletter we discussed earlier, another tool you may want to consider creating is a professional career web site—whether you're in transition or not. A career web site can take several forms, depending on how technically inclined you are and how often you'll want to update it.

A career web site can take several forms, depending on how technically inclined you are and how often you'll want to update it.

One option is a static web site, which can act as an online repository for several of your Job Search Survival Toolkit documents, such as your professional biography, accomplishment stories, and resume. This type of web site is built once and remains fairly static, requiring the least amount of maintenance or updating. You may want a professional web designer or friend who knows the Web to set up a web site for you. Other options include using template-based, type-and-go web sites available from online providers such as GoDaddy (www.godaddy.com) and Network Solutions (www.networksolutions.com). Another excellent resource is VisualCV (www.visualcv.com), which lets you build a professional-looking web presence around your resume and credentials. The best part about VisualCV is that the service is free.

At the other end of the spectrum, if you want to keep things extremely simple and easy to update whenever you like, consider setting up a blog for your career transition. The word "blog" is short for "web log," and it can act as both an online journal and a venue in which to share your professional expertise, opinions, and resources. The leading blog software, Blogger (www.blogger.com), is free, very simple to set up, and is owned by Google. Another popular blogging tool is TypePad (www.typepad.com).

On the following page are examples of both a career web site and a simple career blog.

Sample: Career Transition Web Site

Bob Winters, MBA Subscribe Articles Resume Contact

More Bob

- Bob's BLOG
- Executive Profile
- Career Highlights
- Distinctions
- Subscribe to Bob's mini-newsletter
- Articles by Bob
- Press
- email Bob

About Bob...

Bob Winters has a proven track record and passion for developing great customer experiences:

- Rare combination of leadership ability, technical savvy, and people development skills
- Multiple industry experience including retail, high tech, travel, financial, and distribution
- High profile business to consumer, and complex business to business experience
- Direct sales, customer service, and information technology positions
- Ranked in top 15% of over 7000 executives assessed by Personnel Decisions International (PDI)

Sample: Career Transition Blog

50. Beyond Monster.com: Making the Most of the Web When No One's Hiring

In addition to creating a simple career web site or job search blog, you should also give some thought to what my colleague Eric Kramer calls Online Identity Optimization (OIO). Due to the flood of electronic resumes and the ability to easily search the entire Internet, companies and recruiters are becoming more proactive in searching out top candidates, rather than waiting for good candidates to contact them. The question is: when companies and recruiters search to find good candidates with your experience and expertise, how likely is it that they will find *you*?

When no one's hiring, having a strong web presence is a great way to differentiate yourself. You'll stand out as a technology-savvy, smart self-marketer. Surveys by job placement firms show that recruiters like candidates whose online identity reflects a professional image, well-rounded skills, and a personality that fits their clients' corporate cultures.

When no one's hiring, having a strong web presence is a great way to differentiate yourself. You'll stand out as a technology-savvy, smart self-marketer.

There are numerous ways to become more visible on the Internet—some as simple as developing a free page on a networking web site like Facebook (www.facebook.com) or LinkedIn (www.linkedin.com). More complex tactics include building your own web site optimized for drawing keyword-targeted traffic. Once you decide on your level of interest, effort, and investment, you can establish an OIO strategy that will significantly enhance your online presence.

Here are some effective strategies for increasing and improving your OIO, as recommended by career expert Eric Kramer:

1. **Own your name.** The first strategy is to own your name. Go to a domain registrar such as GoDaddy (www.godaddy.com) or Register (www.register.com), and for less than $10.00, register a domain in your name—www.yourname.com. Note: your name may already be registered, particularly if you have a common name. If this is true in your case, try registering a domain with

your middle name or middle initial. Once you have a "your name" domain, you can build a web site, establish an online career portfolio, or create a blog, all of which will be easily searchable by your name.

2. **Refine and expand your online networking.** Having an extensive list of professional contacts is a well-established job search and career management strategy. Moving your contact list online, establishing a visible (searchable) professional profile, and expanding your network are important OIO strategies. The larger and more established networking sites makes this quick and inexpensive. In fact, most are free. Today, some of the best web sites for professionals are LinkedIn (www.linkedin.com) and Zoominfo (www.zoominfo.com). Facebook (www.facebook.com) and MySpace (www.myspace.com) are also moving toward providing a more professional presence. Once you have registered on these web sites, develop a robust and professional profile. Your online profile is every bit as important as your paper resume in today's world—perhaps more so. Also, look for helpful tools that will identify how you are connected to jobs in which you are interested, and how to quickly upload and link to contacts in your contact management software.
3. **Upgrade your resume to the online world.** Posting your text resume online at major job sites is still important, but it is no longer sufficient for a good OIO strategy. Internet technology enables your career management strategy to include a visual and engaging portfolio about your career. This portfolio includes and supplements your printed resume. A comprehensive web portfolio can include your work history (including links to the companies for which you've worked), significant career achievements, links to articles, presentations, case studies, recommendations, references, awards, and so on. Also, by using graphics, video, and audio, your portfolio will become a more engaging representation of your skills, experience, and work history. Check out VisualCV (www.visualcv.com) for an excellent online portfolio web site.
4. **Write your way to the top.** In the online world, an individual has to establish a virtual self and a home base from which to connect to others. Either a blog or a web site is the most powerful vehicle to develop a recognizable personality, and it provides a home base from which you can initiate your connections. Profiles on social networking web sites can also achieve this goal. However, social

networking web sites are getting very crowded, so it is difficult to stand out. Once you establish a web site or a blog, it must be constantly updated (Google likes fresh, new information). Blogs and web sites with stale, outdated information won't do much for your online identity.

5. **Keep your online identity clean.** A 2008 ExecuNet survey found that 35 percent of recruiters had ruled out job candidates based on what they found on a Google search. Be constantly vigilant about what you do that may end up online, and about what you actually do online. Recently, an executive was visiting his son at college. He was walking by a frat house and impulsively drank a beer from a beer bong (a long tube with a funnel at one end and the drinker at the other end). One week later, his beer bong picture appeared online, and it eventually came back to haunt him. Once a picture gets loose on the Internet, it is virtually impossible to remove it. In today's camera-on-every-phone society, one constantly has to be cautious. Similarly, think of the possible repercussions of articles you write, e-mails you send, blogs to which you contribute, and newsgroups in which you participate. Anything you write online becomes permanent, and when someone searches your name, this information will be found.
6. **Track your OIO strategy.** A simple, quick, and free way to evaluate your OIO strategy is to set up a Google alert to notify you each time your name is found on the Internet (www.google.com/alerts). Simply list your name in an alert, and Google will send you an e-mail message when it finds your name online. How often are you found today? Over time, are you being found more often? When you Google yourself, how high up in the listings are you found? Does your OIO move you up in those listings? These are effective methods to monitor and measure your own OIO.

Your online identity is a form of capital, much like your intellectual capital, financial capital, or social capital (your network). It can be acquired, earned, diminished, damaged, or lost. As is true with the other forms of capital, your online identity is a critical part of your ongoing career management strategy. And, similar to your other types of capital, your online identity can be grown slowly and steadily over time, which will produce the positive results you want. The time to start accumulating and managing your OIO capital is now.

> Your online identity is a form of capital, much like your intellectual capital, financial capital, or social capital.

51. An Outstanding Resume Is Not Difficult to Create—If You Know the Code

I have good news: resumes are not that difficult to put together. There are hundreds of resume books out there, with at least 50 different ways to write resumes "the right way." But after 15 years of experience as a senior-level career coach, I can tell you that there *is* a secret code for resumes—and either you know it, or you don't.

If you *don't* know the code, you will:

- Read a lot of resume books and try several different formats for your resume.
- Listen to every person who offers their expert opinion on resumes (and make every editorial change they suggest).
- Make the even more serious mistake of trying to create your own format from scratch.
- Never be sure if your resume was the disqualifying factor when you *don't* get the offer.

If you *do* know the code, you will:

- Immediately be recognized as someone who is business-savvy and knows the game of professional career search.
- Present your credentials in the best possible light, with a resume that highlights the real value you offer.
- Make it much easier for the recipient to put you in the yes pile rather than the no pile.

I'm going to suggest a fairly radical approach to helping you create a great resume—no theory, no gimmicks, no heavy lifting. Just look carefully at the examples starting on page 107. The easiest way for you to create a top-notch resume is to take exactly what you see in these examples, and do some editing, adapting, and reformatting. Make your own resume match the overall style, tone, and appearance of these samples. Why? Because these formats have been proven to work very, very well—generating an unusually high number of interviews and job offers. It's actually easier than a lot of career professionals (and resume writing services) would have you believe. But, let's be clear. Even though the resume itself can't get you the job, your resume still has to be *exceptional*. Not good, not fine—*exceptional*.

> The main reason that creating a top-notch resume is important is that it improves your thinking.

Why is the resume so important? Simple. The main reason that creating a top-notch resume is important is that it improves your thinking, so you'll be better prepared to market yourself effectively. You only have one chance to make a first impression. Remember that the resume's primary purpose is to get you in the door for an interview. Approach your resume as you would any basic sales and marketing document. You want to sell your way into the interview—by promoting your accomplishments, your credentials, your potential contributions, and your professionalism.

52. You Can Package a Strong Resume in Many Formats

The first decision you need to make is which type of resume best suits your needs. There are three basic options to choose from. None of these is intrinsically right or wrong; they are simply different ways to package your experience and qualifications. Obviously, some resume styles will fit your circumstances better than others, so you'll need to choose your own format carefully.

Here are your three options, along with their respective pros and cons:

- **Chronological.** The chronological resume is the most common type of resume. Because it's arranged by time, a chronological resume is the easiest to organize and write. It's also the easiest to read (which is another plus in the sales and marketing process). The chronological resume is the standard, tried-and-true resume format, which I recommend to 95 percent of my clients. A chronological resume is the right choice when (1) you're continuing in the same occupation and/or industry; (2) your career shows a clear pattern of increasing levels of responsibility; and (3) your employment history has no significant gaps. **Cons:** Any gaps in your work history will be obvious. Limited work experience can also be very apparent. And if past jobs don't tie in directly to the type of positions you're seeking now, or if you're changing careers completely, it may be tougher to sell your capabilities to a new employer using the chronological resume.

- **Functional.** The functional resume organizes your accomplishments into distinct functional areas (hence, the name functional). Use the functional resume only if: (1) you've been a frequent job changer; (2) you're reentering the workforce after an absence of many years; (3) you're in the midst of a significant job or career shift; or (4) you've been at the same job for most of your career. Instead of having job titles as main headings, this style of resume is organized by functions or general areas of expertise. In a typical functional resume, dates are downplayed. **Cons:** Employers tend to be wary of applicants who present this type of resume. They may suspect that the candidate is trying to cover up gaps in his or her work background, or attempting to hide the fact that his or her experience is not directly relevant to the new position's responsibilities.
- **Chronological/Functional Combination.** A combination resume uses elements of both the chronological and functional formats. You can highlight your best accomplishments up-front, and later show a chronological transition from one career step to the next, including job responsibilities. **Cons:** In many ways, this format is the trickiest of the three. Building a sequential timeline of *what* you did and *when* might prove confusing to the reader, even though you're providing dates for everything. Pay special attention to readability and layout issues with this resume format.

To get started, don't develop a resume—develop your resume's building blocks. Regardless of format, every resume will be composed of some standard sections. Following is a list of the main elements that should be included in every resume:

To get started, don't develop a resume—develop your resume's building blocks.

- **Contact Information.** Always include your full name, street address, phone number, and e-mail address, as well as a fax number and cell phone number if you have them.
- **Summary.** A brief statement of who you are, where you're coming from professionally, and what skills and expertise you have to contribute to an organization. Write five or six lines, maximum. This will target and focus the reader on where you might fit into the big picture of their organization. Targeted and specific is better than general and vague. The content of your summary must be oriented toward the benefits and contributions you offer as a candidate. (You can think of the summary as the headline in a newspaper article. If the readers are captivated by the headline, they'll go on to read the body of the article.)
- **Professional Experience.** Your past jobs, roles, responsibilities, and accomplishments. This is the body of the article and where most employers and recruiters will focus 90 percent of their attention. The information you present here, and how you present it, can decide the fate of your candidacy within about 10 seconds of scanning time. Use good journalism habits, and put the most important or impressive facts *first* within each job. Make your professional experience section visually scannable by using bold headings and bullet points. Be specific and results focused.
  Quantify your results whenever possible, by using percentages, dollar figures, and other hard numbers. Highlight increases in good things (e.g., retention, sales, profit, performance, effectiveness) and decreases in bad things (e.g., turnover, losses, costs, inefficiencies, wasted time). This is no place to be shy. Don't lie or exaggerate, but don't undervalue or overlook your past successes, either.
- **Education.** List the schools you attended, academic degrees attained, and years in which you earned them. (Note: you might choose not to include the dates if you graduated a long time ago.) Include the type of degree, major, and any honors or special achievements. Generally speaking, the longer you've been out of school and the more work experience you have, the less important this information is to an employer.

For the last section of your resume, there are several options. Here are some possibilities:

- Professional Development
- Affiliations and Memberships

- Related Experience
- Honors and Awards
- Certification and Licensure
- Publications and Presentations
- Community Service
- Military

In this final section, you'll include only work-related professional development activities, memberships in associations, trade groups and professional societies, leadership positions in industry-recognized organizations, as well as any additional certifications, accreditations or designations you've earned since leaving school. If you don't have a college degree, the professional development seminars and workshops you've participated in—along with any certifications you've earned—will take on special importance here.

Many clients have asked about including an Objective at the top of the resume. I advise them not to do this, for two reasons. First, unless you clearly state otherwise, the reader will automatically assume that you're seeking an opportunity at the next level of the field you're already in. Second, the objective is much better addressed in your cover letter, wherein you can easily tailor your comments to a specific company or position.

Here are some quick guidelines to keep in mind as you develop your resume:

1. Be brief (less is more).
2. Be specific (quantify your results whenever possible).
3. Be active (at the beginning of every sentence, use strong action verbs—see list below).
4. Be selective (focus on information that is truly *relevant* to your career goal, and edit out the rest).
5. Be honest (never, *ever* lie on a resume). If you lie, you'll *always* lose in the long run.

Using these guidelines and the sample resumes on the following pages, create your own effective selling resume, in order to get people interested in meeting with you. If you find that your resume isn't getting the results you want, change it. Your resume is a living document that will be edited and updated throughout your job search, and it will continue to evolve over the course of your entire career.

> Strong action verbs make for a powerful resume.

One of the biggest secrets to an effective resume is also one of the simplest: strong action verbs make for a powerful resume. Use the following table to select the most appropriate action verbs to describe your skills, experiences, accomplishments, and results:

Accelerated
Accomplished
Achieved
Assembled
Budgeted
Built
Compiled
Completed
Consolidated
Converted
Coordinated
Created
Cut
Delivered
Designed
Developed
Directed
Doubled
Earned
Edited
Eliminated
Generated
Implemented
Improved
Increased
Initiated
Installed
Introduced
Launched
Led
Managed
Negotiated
Operated
Organized
Originated
Performed
Planned
Prepared
Produced
Promoted
Provided
Purchased
Reconciled
Recorded
Redesigned
Reduced
Reorganized
Researched
Revised
Scheduled
Simplified
Solved
Staffed
Started
Streamlined
Strengthened
Succeeded
Supervised
Systematized
Traced
Tracked
Trained
Trimmed
Tripled
Uncovered
Unified
Won
Wrote

Sample: Chronological Resume #1

Mandy Morris

5220 Rodeo Drive,
Los Angeles, CA 93821
E-mail: Mandy_Morris846@hollywood.net

Home: (555) 444-6666
Cell: (555) 666-1515

Summary

Accomplished Project Management Professional with extensive experience leading large strategic projects of multinational scope and responsibility. Consistently develops professional relationships with key executives, leading to successful partnerships. Able to craft efficient solutions that achieve business goals. Establishes deep trust, resulting in sustained business success. Areas of expertise include:

- Strategic Executive Management of Large Organizations
- Solid Leadership Experience with Strategic Planning and Execution
- Service Oriented Producer Skilled at Consultative Business Development
- Collaborative Change Motivator with Highly Developed Interpersonal Skills
- Dynamic Leader who Delivers Extraordinary Results

Professional Experience

Moribund Business Associates, Los Angeles, CA **2001–present**

Principal

Founded and managed a consulting services company, providing strategic planning, business process design, and enterprise performance management implementation and execution support.

- Establishing initial client base. Built relationships with three major clients billing more than $10,000 per month and a pipeline of over $1 million.
- Developed and executed sales and marketing programs for delivery of strategic execution and change management programs in small to mid sized organizations.
- Designed recruiting process, resulting in a 25% increase in product placements within six months.

VisionPartners, Inc., Los Angeles, CA **2000–2001**

Principal Solutions Consultant

Developed consulting services programs for a pre-IPO software company, providing an executive management decision support system for collaborative enterprise performance management. Supported a consultative selling approach to business acquisition. Directed consulting services delivery to midsize to large companies.

- Generated $1.4 million in pipeline growth, representing 2,500 users and up to $3 million in revenue.
- Developed and implemented consulting services management practices for on-time and correct delivery of strategic systems implementations.
- Defined sales engagement approach for delivery and implementation of business performance tracking in conjunction with strategic planning and execution.
- Negotiated contracts with C-level positions. Designed contracting process as part of the sales methodology.
- Provided strategic management consulting to executive teams for operational success.
- Developed marketing programs including seminar sales and consultative sales approaches in support of product sales.

RND Corporation, Los Angeles, CA **1998–2000**

Regional Manager

Provided general management and direction of professional services in the Western United States for process manufacturing software company. Led teams of up to 15 people. Managed sales of services to C-level positions.

- Managed ten accounts, representing a combined sales revenue totaling $29.5 million.
- Personally generated revenue of $2.5 million.
- Resolved problem accounts with a history of nonpayment and potential litigation.

(*Continued*)

- Developed a benchmarking and Business Process Reengineering (BPR) practice in conjunction with enterprise business systems implementation.
- Built BPR practice nationally. Added $3.35 million revenue potential. Ensured on-time and correct engagement delivery.

Software Associates, Inc., Los Angeles, CA **1997–1998**
Senior Consulting Manager
Sold and delivered consulting services. Supported product sales activity. Managed programs for implementation of SA software in large manufacturing organizations. Recruited and led consulting teams for long term multi-plant, multinational projects.

- Increased service sales by $6 million, driving sales relationships at the C-level.
- Served as Program Manager for a $1.2 billion organization with 14 plants and 68 sales offices in eight countries.
- Managed a $3 billion project with over 12,000 personnel at five plants in four countries worldwide.
- Led end-to-end supply chain integration. Significantly reduced inventory and carrying costs while improving inventory accountability 30%.

SSA, Inc., Los Angeles, CA **1994–1997**
Senior Applications Consultant
Supported the marketing and delivery of consulting services. Managed projects for implementation of BPCS software and MRP II processes in larger manufacturing organizations.

- Increased sales by $8 million in best year.
- Directed teams of up to 150 people.
- Led business process reengineering effort of a 5-plant high volume paperboard container manufacturer.

Schmendrick Consulting, Los Angeles, CA **1993–1994**
Manager, Business Systems Consulting
Developed a practice to provide strategic planning, process re-engineering, enterprise systems analysis and design, and implementation consulting services to manufacturing companies.

- Led teams of up to 30 people for business consulting to manufacturing and distribution clients.
- Corrected inventory control problem in a $300 million operation, resulting in a savings of 42%.
- Designed open systems solution to $700 million agricultural products manufacturer and distributor. Resulted in significant improvement in system efficiency and integrity.
- Directed assessment in the implementation of changes in a closed loop MRP II at a $70 million per year high tech printer company. Resulted in reorganization and performance improvements.

EDUCATION

M.B.A., University of Central Ipswich, MIS and Finance

B.S., State University of Nevada, MIS

PROFESSIONAL CERTIFICATIONS

CPIM – Certified: Production and Inventory Management

APICS – Certified: Top, Middle and Line Management MRP II

Sample: Chronological Resume #2

Alan S. Rotelle

710 Rodney Circle
Glen Mills, PA 19407

Phone: (222) 888-4444
E-mail: alrot@charter.net

Summary

Award-Winning Creative Director with extensive experience in advertising and marketing communications, in both corporate and agency environments. Proven leader possessing outstanding management and conceptualization skills for creating the proper image to promote growth in sales and profits. Specific areas of expertise include strategic planning, creative development, public relations, media, promotion, and market research.

Professional Experience

Big Bob's Family Markets, Tulpehocken, VA **2001–2009**
Vice President, Creative Marketing
Directed all marketing aspects of 40-store supermarket chain. Supervised professional support staff of 12 people, including Manager of Customer Loyalty, Manager of Advertising Services, Coordinator of Public Relations, Coordinator of Consumer Affairs, and customer shopping and delivery representatives.

- Repositioned company identity, image, and advertising theme as largest family-owned and operated supermarket chain in central VA, resulting in increased share of market in 2002 supermarket report.
- Generated annual savings of more than $350,000 through contract negotiations in first year.
- Doubled in-home print advertising impressions through weekly circular activity during key promotional periods, creating a measurable increase in consumer awareness of Big Bob's.
- Directed strategic action steps on customer loyalty card program, resulting in 10% increase in customer participation.
- Restructured media program to create 40% greater reach and frequency of target customers.

Fuimano's Supermarkets, Watkins Glen, PA **1997–2001**
Director of Creative Services
Planned, developed, and directed execution of all communications. Managed Director of Advertising Services in development of weekly circulars, newspaper, and print advertising with staff of graphic designers. Supervised Director of Media and Promotional Services in planning and executing advertising budgets, broadcast and print media, and sponsorship promotions.

- Appointed Keeper of the Fuimano's Image by the CEO, setting the stage for continued growth in sales and profit and eventual sale of the company to Unilever in 4th quarter 2000.

(*Continued*)

- Directed IT in revamping all reporting and request procedures of Fuimano's Community Cash Back and Corporate Giving Programs, saving company $500,000 annually.
- Served as spokesperson for all media, community relations, and public affairs activities, creating an image as the #1 supermarket in the region.
- Led development of most comprehensive advertising campaign in company's history, resulting in record sales growth.

Rotelle Advertising and Marketing, Ardmore, PA **1985–1997**
Owner and Creative Director
Founded and managed full-service advertising and marketing agency, serving such clients as Fuimano's Supermarkets, Cardinal Soup Company, Mrs. Beck's Foods, Richard Brands, Wally's Chocolates, and other consumer goods manufacturers and retailers.

- Formulated Fuimano Pride theme with subsequent 15 years of campaigns, as well as a host of consumer and employee programs for Fuimano's.
- Created award-winning package design for Richard Brands' Kid's novelty product line, as recognized by Candy Wholesaler and Confectionery magazines.
- Designed award-winning and innovative foodservice sales presentation materials for Mrs. Beck's Foods, as recognized by Philadelphia Advertising Club Addy Awards.

Manly Man Stores, Summit, NJ **1983–1985**
Associate Director, Marketing and Design
Managed advertising agency and separate public relations firm in development and creative execution of all advertising and public relations activities for this men's clothing retail chain, including both consumer and corporate marketing campaigns.

- Created major image turnaround, from local neighborhood retailer to recognized brand of business apparel.
- Developed marketing strategy for regional growth and multimarket expansion, resulting in a 38% increase in company revenue within nine months.

Education

Goober University, Allentown, PA
Bachelor of Business Administration

Affiliation

- Member, Philadelphia Advertising Club, Board of Governors
- Member, American Marketing Association
- Member, Food Marketing Institute, Communications Committee

Sample: Functional Resume #1

William Kimmelblatt

392 Mobius Street
Delran, NJ 08319
williamk22@yahoo.net
555-619-8462 (C) 555-566-1121 (H)

Summary

Operations Management Professional with more than 15 years' experience supervising product development, regulatory affairs, and distribution, with extensive background in quality control. Primary qualifications in the processed food industry. Specific areas of expertise include:

- Recognized as a strategic thinker and problem-solver among peers, employers, and industry associations.
- Demonstrated expertise in all aspects of nutrition, food regulations, and food safety.
- Unique combination of scientific, operations, and management skills.
- Outstanding track-record in consensus management and team building.

Functional Areas of Expertise

Consumer Affairs:

- Guided the restructuring of Company's consumer affairs department into an award-winning brand management resource within 6 months.
- Established Company's "sensitive complaint" system, decreasing corporate response time by 50%, and assuring rapid response to all consumer complaints with health or safety issues.

Regulatory Affairs and Product Safety:

- Conceived, established, and directed corporate and local crisis management teams worldwide, in response to increased product tamperings and other forms of terrorism.
- Avoided negative publicity and prevented loss of inventory and interruptions to operations by resolving more than 26 complex regulatory and government compliance issues.

Legislative Affairs:

- Developed responsive legislative positions for the food industry as Chairman of the Food Manufacturers of America (GMA).
- Guided lobbying efforts through Company's Philadelphia office, involving Food Safety Legislation and FTC's proposed Nutrition Advertising Guidelines.

Scientific and Technical Affairs:

- Directed efforts of four different corporate divisions in scientific and technical matters, concerning product safety, nutrition, and health.
- Managed worldwide quality assurance for all company subsidiaries.

(Continued)

Professional Experience

MURTON INDUSTRIES, Berlin, NJ **1998–2006**

Corporate Director, Quality Assurance (2001–2006)

Decentralized quality control and established a worldwide Corporate Quality Assurance function reporting directly to the President.

Vice President, Morgan Institute of Research (1998–2001)

Supervised Quality Assurance, Regulatory Affairs, and Product Standards, spanning all subsidiaries worldwide.

YAK FOOD CORP., Manfred, MA **1993–1998**

Director, Regulatory and Technical Public Affairs

Managed regulatory and technical matters, including product labeling, product safety, public and scientific affairs in nutrition, health, and food safety for all products.

NORSON FOODS, Miami, FL **1977–1993**

Manager, Regulatory Coordinator (1988–1993)

Authored a benchmark study on the impact of government regulation on P&G's innovative capacity. Presented the research in 16 countries, winning seven prestigious industry awards.

Manager, Regulatory Relations, Folger Coffee (1985–1988)

Directed regulatory affairs, health, safety, and toxicology for the Folger Division.

Various R&D and Manufacturing Staff Assignments (1977–1985)

Education

B.S., New York Center of Technology, New Fane, NY
Major: Food Science

Trade Associations

American Frozen Food Institute
National Food Processors Association
Grocery Distributors of America
Diet and Health Task Force

Professional Affiliations

American Grocer's Association, Senior Member
American Chemical Institute, Associate Member
Association of Food and Drug Officials, Associate Member
Food and Drug Law Committee, Member
Institute of Chemical Technologists, Member
New York Academy of Food Science, Member

Sample: Chronological/Functional Resume

Carol D. Barnes

2632 Parma Road, Apt. J
Aspinwall, PA 18608
E-mail: cdb222@fast.org

Home (555) 555-7825
Mobile (555) 555-7491

Career Summary

Senior Management and Operations Professional experienced in a broad range of facilities and property management functions and business services. With more than 20 years' experience, work history demonstrates a pattern of continued growth, managing many complex projects requiring strong leadership, problem solving, communication, and organization skills. Demonstrated proficiency in the use of all major computer systems and various business and CIKT software applications.

Significant Accomplishments

- Planned, coordinated, and implemented major reallocations of office space. Projects included identification of feasible space (owned and leased), lease negotiations, programming, interior specifications and retrofit, construction, and relocation. Scope of projects ranged up to $2 million budgets, 700 employees and 250,000 square feet. Projects consistently completed on time and under budget.
- Served on a $66 million office building construction project team, providing expertise in practical design, space planning, finishes and specifications, building operations, general services, furniture, and space standards. Coordinated complex installation and interface of new and existing furnishings, as well as phased relocation of 650 employees over a three-month period. Served as primary decision maker and key negotiator in the furniture bid process for a $4 million contract. Recently assumed similar role on $76 million expansion of a research and development facility.
- Consistently met short- and long-term departmental and company strategic goals relating to the development of cost-effective facility standards through demonstrated excellence in leadership and team-building.
- Researched, developed, and implemented CIKT systems of integrated software packages for use in facilities management, space planning, and design processes. Developed and implemented effective furniture tracking systems, integrating CIKT database with Bar Coding for inventory volume of $10 million.

Professional Experience

DOREY PHARMACEUTICALS, INC., Pittsburgh, PA **1984–Present**

Associate Director of Facilities Administration, 2001 to Present

Manage a broad range of facilities, property management and real estate functions, including general maintenance, cleaning, waste management, foodservice, and coordination of security. Supervise a staff of 44 people, numerous contractors, over 1.2 million square feet of office, manufacturing and research space, and an annual budget in excess of $14 million.

(*Continued*)

Manager Facilities Administration, 1994 to 2001

Directed organizational and functional development of an effective facilities department, including real estate, space planning, space inventory, interior design, space standards, and continued responsibilities for office service function.

Manager Office Services, 1990 to 1994

Expanded scope of Supervisor position, adding responsibility as landlord/tenant liaison for 300,000 square feet of leased space. Selected, negotiated, and provided final approval for contract services.

Supervisor Office Services, 1984 to 1990

Directed all building and general services, including maintenance, housekeeping, and waste removal for more than 500,000 square feet, in-house printing, mail and courier operations, business relocation services, office equipment, furniture, and records (archives) center.

ICOGRAPH CORPORATION, Harrisburg, PA **1979 to 1984**

Manager Office and Fleet Services

Supervised mailroom operations, building services, office furniture, equipment supplies, office space planning, telecommunications, and corporate fleet of approximately 500 vehicles. Developed vehicle standards and training programs for division's fleet procedures and driver safety.

Education

Completing Bachelor's Degree in Management, Penn State University

Concurrently pursuing DISR and ESF Certifications

Associate's Degree in Business, Pittsburgh Community College, 1988

Affiliations

ETSL – Professional Member since 1989

CFMG – One of 20 founding members who formed the association, and was later voted to become Pittsburgh Chapter President

Professional development

Internal - Essentials of Management Series
- Communications
- Selective Interviewing
- Decision Making/Problem Solving
- Management Methods
- Performance Appraisals
- Management Processes
- EEO Methods/Legality

External - Tradeline Facilities Programs
- ASA Space Planning Concepts
- ASA Electronic Records Management
- ASA Laser Technology in Records Management

53. How to Use a Resume Addendum

Sometimes, you want to include additional information that either doesn't fit or doesn't make sense to include it in the body of your resume. In those rare cases, the best strategy is to use a resume addendum. This document conveys additional information, related experience, or extra credentials that you want to communicate to a prospective employer.

> The resume addendum conveys additional information, related experience, or extra credentials that you want to communicate to a prospective employer.

Usually, this type of material would be shared late in the interview process, when you feel that you need to pull out all the stops. Obviously, there is an upside and a downside to using this tool, since it's not standard, but the very fact that you're sending a little something extra can be enough to give the impression that you are extra-qualified, extra-interested, or extra-prepared. This is often all it takes to separate you from a crowded field of candidates who are going after the same opportunities. On the following page you'll find a good example of what a resume addendum looks like.

54. The Most Obvious Ways to Find a Job Are Usually the Biggest Wastes of Time

You've just spent a lot of time preparing, strategizing, and developing tools. Now, you're finally ready to get into action. What's the first thing you're likely to do? Go online (or open a newspaper or trade publication) to start scanning the job postings and help-wanted ads. You need to send out as many resumes as you can, as quickly as possible, right? Wrong!

> Most job seekers focus far too much time and energy on Internet job postings and help-wanted ads.

Most job seekers focus far too much time and energy on Internet job postings and help-wanted ads. When the job market is tight and no

Sample: Resume Addendum

Gary Hamel, M.S.

777 Biscuit Bay Highway
Hagersville, MD 20250
Cellular: (555) 111-2222

Home: (555) 999-9999
Fax: (555) 999-8888
E-mail: ghamel77@comcast.org

Related Experience

Health Systems Pharmacy
Part-Time Positions:
Jacob Javits University Hospital, Baltimore, MD **1997–2008**
Clinical Staff Pharmacist
George Washington University Hospital, Washington, DC **1991–1997**
Clinical Staff Pharmacist

Retail Pharmacy
Staff Pharmacist **1985–1991**
Full and part-time experiences at independent and chain retail pharmacies throughout Maryland and the metropolitan Washington, DC area.

Experience with the following pharmacy software systems:

- Health Business Systems, Inc. (HBS)
- Transaction Data Systems (Rx30)
- RCG PharmAssist 3.0

Professional Affiliations

Academy of Managed Care Pharmacy
American College of Clinical Pharmacy
American Society of Health-Systems Pharmacists
American Medical Writers Association
Healthcare Marketing and Communications Council
Pennsylvania Pharmaceutical Association
Rho Pi Phi Pharmaceutical Fraternity

one's hiring, these are the *worst* places to look for a job; your probability of success is close to zero. The sad fact is that only one job in ten is ever advertised, and only one in ten *of those* is any good! That leaves about 1 percent of help-wanted ads and job postings that are worthwhile. Newspaper ads represent the bottom of the job-seeking barrel: entry-level opportunities, high-turnover jobs, and straight-commission sales positions. This means that only 1 percent of good jobs are ever advertised—jobs for which 100 percent of your competition is also applying.

With the advent of the Internet, the whole help-wanted world changed forever. Job board web sites now number in the thousands, with more popping up every day. While these web services have improved the convenience and efficiency of finding job postings, unfortunately the quality of the listings—and the results you can expect from them—are usually very poor. And yet, every job seeker seems to spend many hours sending resumes into this online black hole, hoping that maybe one, just one, of their resumes will land on the right person's desk and generate the interview they've been dreaming of.

If responding to advertised job postings is clearly the least effective job-seeking method, what's a job seeker to do? When you learn of a specific job opportunity at one of your target companies (in this case, through a help-wanted ad or job posting), spend the bulk of your time on the other, more productive methods of learning about that position.

See the following list of strategies for some good suggestions. Don't answer *all* of the help-wanted ads and job postings that are related to your background and qualifications. Instead, answer only a select few. When you do respond to an opening, follow these guidelines:

- Give yourself a limit of two hours per week (about 5 percent of your time) to read and respond to help-wanted ads and job postings, and select only the top five or ten.
- Find someone through your network who works at (or used to work at) the company, or at least knows a lot about it.
- Ask probing questions about the company, and determine if it would be a good fit for your background and preferences.
- If it is a good fit, network yourself to the appropriate hiring manager (not Human Resources!), and try to schedule an appointment.
- In the meeting, focus on the company's needs and challenges, and explain how your related accomplishments could be of direct help.

Of course, this approach requires that you have the right career tools, that you've practiced your interviewing skills, and that you can bring some finesse to the process. Although these strategies don't work every time, when they do work, you can really win big. And it sure beats sending a resume to Human Resources, where it will probably wind up buried in a pile of other resumes.

While it is tempting to sit at your computer all day hitting the send button, this is really the laziest way to search for a new opportunity. Try to view the help-wanted ads and online job postings merely as indicators or hints of where the opportunities are, and then concentrate on actively leveraging your network to get you inside for a meeting with the hiring managers.

While it is tempting to sit at your computer all day hitting the send button, this is really the laziest way to search for a new opportunity.

55. Write Your Own Book on Career Success

Well, maybe not a book. But you should certainly create your very own job search binder. I've found that there are two types of clients: the ones who create a binder to keep track of all their networking, interviewing, career documents, lists, and contacts in one place—and the ones who don't. Guess which group tends to make more progress, get more interviews, land great jobs more quickly, negotiate better deals, and are much happier once they've landed. Guess which group has much more success in the job market, even when no one's hiring. You guessed it—the binder people.

Think of it as command central for your entire job search campaign. After all, you need to take your career transition as seriously as any *real* job you're ever going to have. Treat it like an actual work project.

Your job search binder will keep you organized and make you much more productive.

People who create and use their job search binder find themselves taking it everywhere they go. They take it to the library, they take it to coffee shops, they take it to networking meetings. Sometimes, they even take it on interviews. It's wise to set up this system early—*before* you need it. *Before* you're drowning in handwritten scraps of paper, notes to yourself on the backs of envelopes, loose business cards of people you've met, and stray Post-it® notes.

Go to your favorite office supply store and get a two-inch, heavy-duty, D-ring binder. Buy a three-hole punch and several sets of colored divider tabs. The following is a suggested list of labels for your tab dividers, as well as a structure with which to organize your job search binder. Adapt it as you see fit:

- Accomplishment Stories
- Positioning/Departure Statements
- Professional Biography
- Target Companies
- Contact List
- Network Contacts
- Professional Reference List
- Letters of Reference
- Resume
- Self-Assessments
- Networking Agenda/Script
- Networking Records and Notes
- Follow-up Tracking System
- Copies of Written and E-mail Correspondence
- Master List of All Jobs You're Actively Pursuing
- Interview Notes
- Articles and Research
- Job Postings
- Recruiters
- Ideas/Miscellaneous Notes
- Inactive Section (don't throw anything away)

Once you've built your job search binder, keep reorganizing it as you make progress and as new opportunities arise. This will serve as your three-dimensional database and job search pipeline, so you'll always know where you stand and what should come next with any prospective opportunity.

56. Every Company Is Hiring All the Time, Even in a Down Economy

It's time for the rubber to meet the road, and for you to knock some doors down. But first, I want to let you in on a big secret that, as a professional career coach for more than 15 years, I can reveal to you now. Here it is: Every company is hiring all the time—as long as *you* have what *they* need.

> Every company is hiring all the time—as long as *you* have what *they* need.

You read that right. Every company. All the time (unless they're about to go bankrupt). What does this mean to *you*? It means you should stop looking for *job openings* and look instead for *needs, problems, and challenges!*

I can't tell you how many times I've had clients shy away from a company on their Target List simply because they heard that the organization is not hiring. Guess what? Almost every time, I've had a slightly bolder client get multiple interviews at that very same organization, negotiate a great compensation package, and land a great job—all at the same time that other candidates were under the impression that "they're not hiring."

The rules of supply and demand are always in play—regardless of the economy, the unemployment headlines, or what your friends say. If you present yourself as a *solution* to a *problem* that's been costing the organization time, money, stress, headaches, and heartaches—and if you deliver your message with clarity, conviction, and reasonable proof (using all the tools in your Job Search Survival Toolkit)—the company will often *create* a spot for you on their team. They can't afford *not* to hire you if that's the case. So always think positive, and don't be turned away as easily as some people might like you to be.

57. A Strong Cover Letter Is Designed to Get You an Interview

You may have noticed that we didn't mention the topic of cover letters until now. There's a reason for that; they are not so much a part of your Job Search Survival Toolkit as they are part of the *implementation* of your overall self-marketing strategy. That's right. A cover letter is a sales presentation in disguise.

A cover letter is a sales presentation in disguise.

At this point in your job hunt, you're reaching out for a very tangible goal—a job interview. Cover letters are the most commonly used method to introduce your credentials to an employer, and they can serve as one of your strongest selling tools.

Avoid the standard, boring types of cover letters that employers receive every day: "I'm very interested in a position with Motley Corporation as a Programming Analyst. Enclosed please find my resume." *Blah, blah, blah*. A letter like this basically says, "Hey, here's my resume and I need a job!" That's not a very impressive sales presentation, is it? More importantly, it does nothing to distinguish you from the crowd of other applicants sending the very same kind of drab, dull attachments with their drab, dull resumes.

58. Cover Letters That Open Doors for Any Situation

There are many times during the implementation of your full search campaign where you'll rely on a cover letter to speak for you. The way you present yourself on paper can make or break your success during any phase of the job search process. Think about all of the different situations in which cover letters might be useful in opening doors, making a strong first impression, and keeping your candidacy on the front burner in the eyes of employers:

- Letter responding to an advertised opening
- Letter following up on a personal referral
- Letter introducing yourself to a decision maker
- Thank-you letter
- Follow-up letter
- Response to a job-offer letter
- And others...

Cover letters (including e-mails) are the delivery method for most of your career communications, and they will almost always accompany the career documents in your Job Search Survival Toolkit.

> Writing cold approach letters (when you don't know anyone at the Target Company) is very ineffective.

There may be some instances when it will be necessary to send a cold letter, but you should try to avoid these cases. Experience has shown repeatedly that the results of cold letter campaigns are extremely disappointing. Frankly, I think these types of letters are a waste of time, energy, and money. Even worse, the low response rate makes job seekers feel terribly disappointed and frustrated.

So, of course you should learn how to write a great cold approach letter, but I urge you to use this type of document as infrequently as you can. Instead, focus on warm job search letters, written to the people to whom you have been referred through your network. And be sure to mention the name of the referring party in the first paragraph of your letter. You'll find that these warm referral letters garner a much higher response rate, and can actually move your search forward.

Rules of Thumb for a Well-Written Cover Letter

No matter what the purpose of your written communication, a good cover letter should:

- Direct the reader's attention toward the *strongest* aspects of your background and qualifications (and away from any weaknesses).

- Customize and personalize your message to each specific company and recipient.
- Highlight and expand upon the most relevant facts on your resume.
- Give new, relevant, customized information that is *not* included anywhere on your resume.
- Show that you know the company well, that you've done your homework, and that you're familiar with the challenges and opportunities in their industry—or better yet, at their organization in particular.

Master the Three Basic Parts of a Cover Letter

A cover letter can be broken down into three basic parts:

Part 1: Introduction. Explain why you're writing to the employer. Did you see an advertisement? Were you referred by a friend or current employee? Have you seen one of their executives present at a conference or meeting? Did you read something in the business press about the company? Be specific and use your research. Give the recipient of your correspondence a sense of your knowledge by referring to industry trends, specific events, or media coverage. This is the best way to demonstrate your interest in the organization and your preparedness.

Part 2: The Sales Presentation. To sell yourself effectively, tell the employer your qualifications and give examples of your related experience. The same elements that make your resume effective will work in your cover letter—use action words; be brief; be specific. Write about your relevant accomplishments, and use facts and numbers to back up your claims.

Part 3: Wrap Up and Close. Be sure to conclude in one sentence what you can do for the organization. Wrap up your letter as strongly as you opened it. Restate your interest in working with the company and why. Genuine interest and enthusiasm, combined with your knowledge of the company, are hard to resist. Close the letter by directly requesting a meeting or interview. Take charge of the process by stating a time frame in which you'll call. Then follow up precisely as promised, to demonstrate how responsible and professional you are.

Here's a typical cover letter for your reference:

Sample: Cover Letter

April 30, 2009

Ms. Estelle Nordberg
President and CEO
Mahvelous Innovations, Inc.
888 Monterey Ave., Building E, Suite 300
Monterey, CA 90210

Dear Ms. Nordberg:

According to last week's *New York Times* piece about Mahvelous Innovations, you're planning on expanding into the stuffed toy market. With your innovative product line and aggressive marketing plan outlined in the article, there's no doubt that your company dominates the domestic toy market. I would like to join such a winning team!

As Creative Director for a small toy manufacturer, I designed and supervised production of a stuffed toy line that represented 32% of our 2008 profits. This was the first time any one toy line generated such a large margin of profitability. In addition, I developed new packaging for the company's entire product offering. Once this new packaging was introduced, sales to toy retailers went up by 24%.

Ms. Nordberg, I would like to produce similar results for Mahvelous Innovations. With my 15 years in the toy industry and my hands-on experience in both product and package design, I know I can contribute a great deal to your design department. With this in mind, I plan to call you next week so we can schedule a mutually convenient time to talk on the phone or meet in person at your offices in Monterey. I am looking forward to speaking with you, and thank you in advance for your consideration.

Sincerely,

Marie Dennis

Enclosure/Attachment

NOTE: Attach or enclose your Professional Biography, *not* your resume, unless there is a specific job opening at the company that matches your qualifications.

The Perfect Match Cover Letter Gets the Best Results

When responding to an advertised opening, following up after a meeting or interview, or expressing an interest in pursuing a specific opportunity arising out of your networking activities, the ideal format for your cover letter is called a perfect match letter. All three of these situations are great opportunities to sell yourself by matching *your* experience, strengths, and contributions to *their* problems, needs, and challenges.

The perfect match letter gets its name from the fact that your letter is formatted into two columns with two headings across the top, giving the body text an overall appearance of a side-by-side matching exercise. The reason this format is so effective is that you're making it very easy for the recipient to see that you're a match for every criteria the employer is looking for. This means that your resume will be placed into the "yes" pile.

Another compelling reason to master this type of letter is the fact that, in my experience, perfect match letters have a 75 percent response rate—even when no one's hiring. That's right—75 percent of the time you send this type of letter, you'll receive a positive response, whether that's a phone call, a meeting with a recruiter, or a screening interview with the hiring manager. The perfect match letter is even more powerful when no one's hiring, because it focuses so strongly on tangible results. When the job market is extremely tight, you can't afford *not* to use this type of cover letter.

> Perfect match letters have a 75 percent response rate—even when no one's hiring.

On the following pages, you'll find some good examples of perfect match letters. The way to create these is to use either tabs, tables, or columns in your favorite word processing program, and format the letter according to the examples you see on the following pages. For the slightly computer-challenged, an alternative format, called the vertical match letter, accomplishes the same goals in an easier-to-create format. The final example in this collection of letters demonstrates the vertical match layout.

Sample: Perfect Match Letter #1

Marie Dennis

530 Trumbull Lane
East Gybip, CA 90520

Cell: (555) 999-8888
Home: (555) 555-7777

E-mail: mariedennis1@sbc.net

Ms. Deanne Schuster
Vice President
SBE Group, Inc.
1005 Trade Plaza, Suite 555
New York, NY 60022

April 30, 2009

Dear Ms. Schuster:

Thank you for meeting with me last week on the recommendation of Sandra Singh. I was happy to learn about the valuable services the your organization offers its members. Your candid comments about the many challenges in fulfilling the group's mission helped me to understand why you have opened a search for a new Business Development Manager.

I am very interested in this leadership opportunity. With my understanding of the position's requirements, I am confident that my proven experience and capabilities would enable me to make outstanding contributions in the following areas:

Your Requirements	**My Contributions**
Revenue growth/business development to attract new members, expand product/service offerings, and build key client relationships.	• Established independent HR consulting practice with multiple service offerings and profitable revenue stream. • Developed new business, building revenues, from zero to $3.03 million in 3 years. • Exceeded revenue goals by 11% in 2000, and 24% in 2001. • Surpassed 2007 targets by 36% in 1997 and 22%. • Increased revenues by 24% in 1994. • Established new projects and strengthened long-term relationships with major clients in a variety of industries.
Leadership and people management, including coaching, mentoring, motivating and leading by example. Performance management experience.	• Recruited, hired, and directed an enthusiastic, motivated team that achieved average customer ratings of 4.7 (on a scale of 1 to 5).

Your Requirements	My Contributions
	• Coached many managers and executives to enhance their leadership skills and value. • Mentored high potential people by providing advice, instruction, observation and feedback. • Established employee performance goals, measurements and rewards designed to collectively achieve organizational goals.
In-depth financial management, with experience developing and controlling budgets. Manage service lines to maximize profitability.	• Achieved profitability in independent consulting practice within eight months. • Produced profit margins of 12% in 2006 and 28% in 2007 (more than double the target). • Reduced salary costs by 25% by creating and implementing a new staffing model. • Analyzed volume and demand (including impact of pricing and marketing) and cost structures for service lines. Designed plans to maximize revenue growth and profitability.

While you indicated that strategic marketing knowledge is a less essential requirement, I believe my background in this area would help me establish credibility with SBE members and staff, and allow me to "hit the ground running." As you know, I possess expertise in many key disciplines of marketing, and a breadth of knowledge in all related areas.

For all of the above reasons, I am confident that I would be an excellent fit for this position, and an invaluable asset to SBE.

Thank you Ms. Schuster for giving me such a complete picture of SBE and this exciting opportunity. I plan to follow-up by phone before the end of the week to schedule our next meeting.

Sincerely,

Marie Dennis

Enclosures/Attachments

Sample: Perfect Match Letter #2

Heather Woodman

150 Rolling Rock Road
Leverington, MA 29991
E-mail: heatherwood1@sbc.net

Cell: (555) 999-8888
Home: (555) 555-7777

Mr. Joe Garagiola
Director of Operations
Modern Postcard, Inc.
777 Sansom Drive
Palo Alto, CA 30210

July 13, 2009

Dear Mr. Garagiola:

Thank you for meeting with me yesterday about my career search. I am so glad that our mutual friend Dick Clifford referred me to you. When we spoke, you discussed various challenges within your supply chain management systems. Additionally, you mentioned your desire to reduce the costs and risks of code customization.

In all of my past positions, I have been tasked with reducing costs and improving processes by analysis and problem solving, resulting in innovative solutions. From our conversations and your job description, you seem to be seeking a person who can accomplish exactly that.

Mr. Garagiola, I am very interested in the Applications Development Manager leadership opportunity. With my understanding of the position's requirements, I am confident that my proven experience and ability would enable me to make outstanding contributions in the following areas:

Opportunity Requirements	**My Qualifications**
Addresses customer complaints and concerns, and works to formulate acceptable resolutions	• Worked closely with user community over the last 15 years as a listener, problem solver, and user advocate.
Maintains personnel schedule	• Utilized Gantt and WBS for projects for IT and client staff, over a period of 12 years.
Identifies and implements process improvements	• Identified process improvements, cost reductions, and process controls. Documented and implemented these initiatives accordingly.

Negotiates contracts	• Negotiated large contracts for telecommunications services, contractors, and hardware vendors. Saved $2.5 million on those expenditures while boosting internal satisfaction numbers by 32%.
Manages and sponsors larger projects	• Proposed and managed various projects and programs of varying sizes, up to $2 million.
Prepares time and cost estimates for completing projects	• Identified and budgeted hardware, software, database, training, documentation requirements, dependencies, and risks for projects.
Responsible for performance of a group	• Consistently created a positive atmosphere and inspire others. Taught courses on improving the understanding and usage of technology.
Responsible for hiring	• Over the last nine years, interviewed hundreds of individuals to build solid teams. Also identified skills and wrote job descriptions for candidates for over four years.
Responsible for management and key development of subordinates	• Trained and mentored, assigned tasks, and monitored progress of all personnel over the last five years.
Directs and coordinates work of others to develop, test, install, and modify programs	• Over the last 11 years, worked in roles of increasing responsibility, managing individuals to complete projects according to budget and plan.
Works with others to improve the corporate condition and IT operations	• Have consistently taken the lead in discussing opportunities to reduce costs and improve IT service levels across the company.

As you know, I possess expertise in many key disciplines of application development and a breadth of knowledge in all related technologies.

For all of the above reasons, I am confident that I would be an excellent fit for this position and an invaluable asset to Modern Postcard, Inc. With this in mind, I plan to call you early next week to schedule an exploratory discussion.

I look forward to speaking with you again soon, Mr. Garagiola, and thank you for your interest.

Sincerely,

Heather Woodman

Enclosures/Attachments

Sample: Vertical Match Letter

Daniel Fischer

26351 Ace Highway
Truro, MA 29741
E-mail: dfischer111@hubnet.org

Cell: (555) 999-8888
Home: (555) 555-7777

Ms. Maureen Mayer
Product Development Director
Transtronics Group, Inc.
1111 Elm Boulevard
Branford, CA 22975

June 12, 2009

Dear Ms. Mayer:

I enjoyed meeting with you last Friday to discuss why I would be a good fit for the Principal Product Manager position. From our conversation, and those with other team members, I feel even more interested in this opportunity with Transtronics. I liked the passion and candor with which everyone spoke to me, and I feel confident that I will be able to work well with all of them.

I have taken the liberty of outlining below several of the requirements you seem to be looking for in the successful candidate, along with my relevant professional accomplishments:

Your Requirement
Eight plus related experience in marketing.

My Qualification
Twelve plus years of marketing experience.

Your Requirement
Able to develop a successful business plan that incorporates all aspects of the marketing mix, including product, price, distribution, promotion and product forecasting, resulting in successful product launches.

My Qualification
Researched and developed business plans that detailed all aspects of the marketing mix, and executed these plans together with other departments, including R&D, regulatory, clinical, sales, finance and operations.

Your Requirement
Define the product feature and benefit roadmap for next generation devices.

My Qualification
Defined new product concepts, features and benefits, and developed benefit roadmap for electronic monitoring devices through market research with R&D engineers.

Your Requirement
Able to make effective presentations to senior management.

My Qualification
10 years experience successfully creating and delivering business presentations to senior management.

Your Requirement
Develop dynamic promotional and educational material to train Sales Representatives.

My Qualification
Developed competitive feature and benefit matrices, brochures, animation, sales tools and research papers for electronic safety devices for Sales Representative training. Also developed comprehensive education programs for both Sales Representatives and Engineers.

Your Requirement
Develop product trouble explanatory information to support Sales Representatives with their damage control efforts.

My Qualification
Created safety monitoring and alarm product recall Q&A information, diagrams and customer letters to explain the nature of the alarm system's trouble and how it was corrected.

Your Requirement
Ability to successfully lead and motivate cross-functional teams.

My Qualification
Led multiple cross-functional teams related to creating a product roadmap, product development market research, creation and engineering of sales tools, etc. Spent 30%+ of my time in the field to motivate and add value to Sales Representatives and customers.

Your Requirement
Experience developing key international markets.

My Qualification
5 years of market development experience overseas in 13 countries, including market research analysis, development of promotional materials, pricing strategies and distribution plans – resulting in successful product launches and revenue growth for multiple electronic product lines.

Ms. Mayer, I genuinely feel that I will be able to add significant value to Transtronics in its effort to develop teams, grow revenues and create next generation products. I sincerely hope that I will have the opportunity to join your team. I will call you early next week to follow-up and discuss next steps. Thank you very much for your consideration.

Best Regards,

Daniel Fischer

Enclosure/Attachment

59. Recruiters Are *Not* in Business to Help You

When the job market gets tight, many people start operating under some false and counterproductive assumptions. Let's make one thing clear right now: Executive search firms, recruiters, and employment agencies are *not* in business to help you land a job. They are not your advocates, they are not your friends, and they are not your agents.

> Executive search firms, recruiters, and employment agencies are *not* in business to help you land a job. They are not your advocates, they are not your friends, and they are not your agents.

Think about it: Your local newspaper is not your advocate or friend, either. And just like a newspaper, recruiters, employment agencies, and executive search firms are merely channels through which you may (or may not) secure an opportunity for an interview. Recruiters and search firms can be quite helpful in your job search, as long as you know how to manage the process. But never forget that they work not for you, but for the organizations that pay them to find qualified candidates.

When you're looking for work in a period of increasing unemployment numbers and decreasing job opportunities, you certainly can't afford to waste any time or money playing games with recruiters and search firms. So, let me offer you a clear picture of how these services operate.

Employment Agencies That Charge You a Fee

Agencies that charge you a fee should be avoided at all costs. These organizations, which generally handle lower-level jobs, collect a fee from *you*, the job seeker, presumably in exchange for arranging interviews with potential employers. They often employ bait-and-switch tactics, in which they post job openings that don't exist, lure you into their office, and then send you on interviews for positions that are not appropriate for you. Worst of all, these agencies may ask you to sign a contract stipulating that if you leave a position they placed you in within a year or less, *you* will be responsible for paying *them* the placement fee they lost (which could be tens of thousands of dollars).

When the employment landscape is bleak, many people get burned by these types of agencies that charge job seekers hundreds or even thousands of dollars in bogus fees. These companies prey on desperate job seekers who are scared by bad economic or employment news, yet they provide almost no real value, services, leads, or resources.

Contingency-Fee Recruiters

Contingency-fee recruiters are paid a fee (a percentage of the salary) only if their client company actually hires a candidate identified by the recruiter. They are generally not paid anything unless a position is filled, and thus their primary business strategy is volume—to handle many assignments, refer as many candidates as possible to potential employers, and place as many people as they can in jobs. They will not typically work closely with you to ensure that a job is the best possible fit for *you*.

Think of contingency recruiters as working strictly on commission and competing directly with other contingency recruiters who are trying to fill the same spots. You must take full responsibility for judging, filtering, and sorting the opportunities suggested by contingency-fee recruiters.

> You must take full responsibility for judging, filtering, and sorting the opportunities suggested by recruiters.

Retained Executive Search Firms

These are the classic *headhunters*, who are given an exclusive right to conduct a search on behalf of their client company. They are usually paid their consulting fee (or at least a portion of it), even if the search is unsuccessful. Executive search consultants usually receive between 25 and 33 percent of the candidate's first year's salary. These types of search consultants generally play a more active and selective role in helping to frame job requirements, prescreening candidates, conducting background and reference checks, and facilitating negotiations.

Even executive search firms *are focused on helping their client company;* they are *not* working for you. It is in the retained search firm's best interest to make sure a candidate is an excellent fit for the position, the industry, the company, and the culture, because this ensures that they'll get additional search contracts from that employer.

Besides being an important source of jobs for more senior candidates, executive search consultants can also be important as networking contacts. They can provide you with information about industry conditions and possible targets, as well as insightful feedback about your campaign strategy. However, never confuse executive search consultants with career coaches; they play very different roles.

> When working with any type of recruiter or executive search firm, maintain control of them and their activities.

As with all facets of the job search process, it is up to *you* to take full responsibility and direct the search. No one will be as invested as you are in conducting a successful search and getting a great job offer. When working with any type of recruiter or executive search firm, maintain control of them and their activities. I tell my clients to supervise the work of recruiters as though they were managing a group of employees. This means following some important guidelines:

- Be careful and selective in choosing which recruiters you want to work with. Politely decline to work with those who don't appeal to you or who are inappropriate for your situation. Note: the best resource for finding and selecting search firms is the Directory of Executive & Professional Recruiters, published by Kennedy Information (www.kennedyinfo.com).
- When dealing with search firms and recruiters, be open and direct about your job objectives, past compensation, desired salary, geographic preferences, and other details. Give them what they need to know to ensure a good fit for you—and a successful assignment for them.
- The first question to ask when you are contacted by a recruiter is, "For whom do you work?" You want to determine immediately if the caller is an *external recruiter* (working for a bona fide search firm) or an *internal recruiter* (such as a human resources specialist). If you learn that the caller works directly for the employer, you must treat them as such, which means *not* providing any information about your current or desired compensation. We'll talk about this more in the section on salary negotiation.
- Never pay any sort of registration fee, representation fee, or other money—for *anything*. All of the recruiter's fees should be paid by the employer.
- When interviewing, make sure that the job is exactly what the recruiter described. Confirm (and reconfirm, if necessary) the

important job details, responsibilities, and expectations. Don't take the recruiter's word for it; ask your own questions about the job, and use your own judgment.

- Remember that you are the source of the recruiter's income (indirectly). This gives you leverage. You are entitled to courtesy and respect, as well as honest and prompt answers to your questions.
- Do not sign any contracts or make any agreements that obligate you to work exclusively with one search firm. This arrangement only benefits the agency and limits your exposure in the marketplace. If you need to review or accept agreements of any kind, be sure to read them carefully and have them reviewed by an employment attorney.
- Ask that your resume and other information not be forwarded to any prospective employer without your prior approval. This is because there may be some companies that you don't want to receive your resume.
- Be sure that the recruiter does not edit or alter your resume in any way without your prior permission.
- Work closely only with a handful of carefully selected search firms.
- At the point of negotiating your compensation for a new position, do not rely on the recruiter to handle this for you. You must either conduct the negotiations yourself or at least be actively involved in the negotiation process.
- Focus only 5 to 10 percent of your job search energies on recruiters. Most of your time should be spent on more productive activities that give you more control (such as professional networking).

Large, national search firms may have offices in many cities, and these offices are generally online with each other and share resources. If you get into their database in one office, your profile will come up in another city if an appropriate opportunity arises that matches your credentials. This may be helpful if you are willing to relocate. Smaller search firms that are locally based may also have excellent reputations in their own geographic areas and certainly should not be overlooked.

You make contact with external search firms and recruiters by sending them your resume with a cover letter. This letter should be very similar to the cold cover letter you would send to a prospective employer. It could be very helpful to introduce yourself to a search firm through a personal referral. Or, better still, offer them a quid pro quo by including phrases in your cover letter along the lines of: "During my years in this industry, I have met many highly qualified professionals. If I can be of any help to you in one of your searches, please don't hesitate to contact me."

60. Interviewing: Psychology, Strategies, Tactics, and Practice

Once you've done your strategic networking, gotten some names and numbers, made some introductions, leveraged recruiters, and gotten referred to the right people in the right places, it's time to sit down and master the art of the interview. Let's start by looking at the phases of the interview process. In some cases, you'll actually be taken through *all* of these interview steps before a hiring decision will be made.

What follows is an outline of the different types of company interviews, how they work, and what you can expect during each of these interview situations. Then, we'll review the specific questions that you should be prepared to answer—and those you should be prepared to *ask*—to maximize your success at every step in the interviewing process.

Types of Interviews

- **Informational:** No specific job under discussion. Purpose is learning about industry, company, people, skills required, cultural fit, and perhaps generating additional avenues of research or more people for you to contact.
- **Screening:** This is the first serious step in the interviewing process. Consider this a "live ammo exercise." Used as the first step to narrow the field of candidates who are being considered for employment. Screening may be done by an outside recruiter or in-house human resources representative. Usually done over the phone.
- **Hiring Manager:** An in-depth look at an applicant to confirm desired requirements and/or technical abilities, motivation, and overall personal and cultural fit with the organization. Typically 60 to 90 minutes in length, conducted by the individual for whom you would be working.
- **Approval:** A series of sequential interviews, sometimes formal and sometimes informal (such as over lunch), conducted by team

members, peers, or colleagues in departments with whom you would interact. Getting to this stage assumes that the hiring manager liked you and passed you along for the team's approval. If everyone on the team gives you the thumbs up, you'll have a good chance of getting a job offer.

- **Group:** A more formal and structured interview, conducted by a panel of three to five peers and the hiring manager (at the same time) to narrow the field of applicants. Sometimes, this involves behavioral interview methods, hands-on tasks, or an assignment to work on a real-time problem that the group is facing. A conference call or video-phone format may be used in long-distance situations.
- **Offer:** Hiring manager or human resources representative formally offers the job to the top choice. Their focus is now to provide you, their top candidate, with information you need to make a decision and enter into a win–win negotiation process. This will result in the best possible deal for both you and the company that wants to hire you.

Interviewing can be best described as two-way storytelling. You need to provide the interviewer with accurate, relevant stories about your career achievements and job performance. The interviewer needs to tell you the story of the company, describe the position in question, and explain specifically how they want *you* to fit into their picture. This will allow both parties to assess their level of interest in the other.

Think about the basic elements of a good story. It always has:

A *beginning*—in the case of an interview, this can be small talk, setting the tone, establishing rapport, and providing a personal connection between you and the interviewer. The key here is to be your best self—don't force anything.

A body or *middle*—this is the substance of the one-on-one information exchange. All your preparation, accomplishment stories, personal strengths, abilities, and value statements can be used here to make a compelling case for yourself.

A strong *ending* or finish—the close makes sure the interviewer has a firm grasp on where you fit into the company's landscape, exactly how you can add value to the position in question, and how you're superior to the other candidates. This part of the story ensures that the interviewer is left with a good impression of you, your track record, and your ability to help the company meet its objectives.

61. Interviewing Survival Guide for When No One's Hiring

The key to acing the interview is preparation, preparation, preparation. No matter which kind of interview you're faced with, there is one and only one key: *preparation*.

One thing I have noticed over the years in my career coaching practice is that candidates often get trapped in certain interview questions that are *designed* to make them say something negative or self-defeating (which generally leads to rejection). Indeed, job seekers are not even aware of how negative many of their answers sound at interviews.

Here's my biggest piece of advice on the subject of interviewing: never state anything negative or anything that could possibly be construed as negative. Candidates can avoid being disqualified by stating all of their answers in positive (or, at least, neutral) terms.

> Never state anything negative or anything that could possibly be construed as negative.

The following are some of the most commonly asked interview questions, along with suggested approaches for answers. It is important that you *prepare* and *practice* these responses (*yes, out loud!*) until you are able to handle all of the questions effectively and naturally, using your own words and infusing your own personality.

Why do you want to work here? How can you help our company? Why should we be interested in you?

Answer is always based on information you've researched in advance about the company and their needs.

Why have you been out of work so long?

A tough question if you've been out of work a long time. You don't want to seem like damaged goods. You want to emphasize factors that have prolonged your job search *by your own choice*.

EXAMPLE: "After my department was eliminated, I made a conscious decision not to jump on the first opportunities to come along. I've found that I can always turn a negative into a positive if I try hard enough. This is what I was determined to do. I decided to take whatever time I needed to think through what I do best, where I could contribute most, the kinds of organizations I'd like to work with, and then identify those companies that could offer such an opportunity. So between my being selective and the companies in our industry downsizing, the process has taken some time. But I'm convinced that when I find the right match, all this careful evaluation will have been worthwhile for both the company that hires me and for me."

If you were choosing someone for this job, what kind of person would you select?

Answer is to state your own general qualifications, without being too obvious or self-serving.

If you could have any job, which one would you want at this company?

Answer should reflect a very general description of the type of role for which you are interviewing—*not a specific title*.

What weaknesses do you have for this job?

TRAP QUESTION. Never state anything negative! Answer is to ponder the question for a while, and then state that you can't think of any weaknesses that would compromise your performance at this job, or that would negatively impact your handling of the job's responsibilities.

What do you expect to get in this job that you haven't gotten in your current/previous job?

TRAP QUESTION. Never state anything negative! State that your current/previous jobs have met or exceeded your expectations. With this new position, you would hope to have broader responsibilities and make greater contributions over time.

What do you see as your future here?

Don't be too specific in your response. State that you would expect to be contributing at higher levels and have increased responsibility over time.

What changes would you make to our company if you came on board?

TRAP QUESTION. This question can instantly derail your candidacy. No matter how comfortable you may feel with your interviewer or the situation, you are still an outsider. No one, including your interviewer, likes to think that a know-it-all outsider is going to come in, turn the place upside down, and promptly demonstrate what idiots everybody at the company has been for years. Here's how you might reply to this question.

EXAMPLE: "I wouldn't be a very good doctor if I gave my diagnosis before examining the patient. If I were hired for this position, I'd want to take a good look at everything you're doing and understand why it's being done that way. I would have in-depth meetings with you and the other key people to get a deeper grasp of what could be improved. From what you've told me so far, the areas of greatest concern to you are. . ." (name them). *Then, do two things*. First, ask if these are, in fact, the major concerns. If so, reaffirm how your experience in meeting similar needs elsewhere might prove very helpful. Second, present specific accomplishment stories that relate directly to the employer's most pressing needs and challenges.

Are you considering other positions at this time?

TRAP QUESTION. Simply say "yes." If you say "no," you'll seem like a loser who nobody else values as an attractive candidate.

How does this opportunity compare to other opportunities you're considering?

"From what I've heard so far, very favorably. . . and I would like to learn more!"

What other companies/opportunities are you looking at now?

"As I'm sure you can appreciate, I'm not at liberty to divulge the identities of the other companies, as I am still in discussions with them. I need to protect their privacy, as I would do for your company under similar circumstances."

What are your short- and long-term goals?

Short range: "To secure an appropriate new position where I can apply my skills and experience to increase the company's productivity and profitability." Long range: "To assume more responsibility and make greater contributions over time for my employer."

What motivates you?

Focus the answer on your core values and also on the priorities of the company you are interviewing with (and how they align). You should have already identified these factors through your up-front research.

Why aren't you earning more money at this stage of your career?

You don't want to give the impression that money is not important to you, yet you want to explain why your salary may be a little below industry standards (if it is).

EXAMPLE: "Making money is very important to me, and one reason I'm here is because I'm looking to earn more. Throughout my career, what's been even more important to me is doing work I enjoy at the kind of company I can respect."

Then get specific about what your ideal position and ideal employer would be like, matching them as closely as possible to the opportunity at hand.

What have you done to improve yourself during the last year?

Talk about professional development, training classes, educational programs, study in your field, on-the-job training, skill-building, and relevant books you've read, etc.

How do you spend your spare time?

Say something inoffensive, apolitical, and innocuous, such as reading, exercise, travel, home projects, gardening, family activities, etc.

Tell me about your health.

Questions about your health and medical status are usually illegal. In most cases, the interviewer is simply unaware that such questions are off-limits. When health-related questions do arise, they are often motivated by the employer's concerns about the cost of health insurance, or to determine if you are physically capable of performing the job's duties. That being said, the best approach is generally to answer the question rather than making an issue of it. Good responses include, "My health is excellent, thank you." Or, "I have no health problems that would prevent me from fulfilling all the responsibilities of this position." If you do have a serious health challenge, it is always best to make this clear at the outset.

What do you look for when *you* hire people?

If you're applying for a management position, it's likely that part of your job responsibilities will include sitting in the *other* chair at some point, interviewing candidates for *your* team. Being unprepared for this question shows a lack of management perspective. For the best answer, weave your comments around the three most important qualifications for any job:

1. *Can* the person do the work (qualifications)?
2. *Will* the person do the work (motivation)?
3. Will the person *fit in* (our kind of team player)?

If you could relive your last 15 years, what changes would you make?

"Nothing is perfect, but overall I would say that I'm quite satisfied with the way my life and career have developed, so I wouldn't make any significant changes."

If you are interviewing for a position that clearly represents a career change, you could add something like, "Looking ahead, I am excited about applying my transferrable skills to this new role."

Tell me about your greatest achievement/disappointment in your life.

Give one *personal* example (like meeting your spouse and getting married, putting yourself through college, saving up to buy your first house, etc.). Then give your best *professional* accomplishment story (make it relevant to the company's apparent needs and challenges). As for the disappointment, give an answer similar to the one above, such as, "Overall, I would say that I'm quite satisfied with the way my life and career have been developing, so I really can't think of any major disappointments."

Why should I hire you?

Believe it or not, this is a killer question, because so many candidates are unprepared for it. If you hesitate or ad lib, you'll blow it. If you know the employer's greatest needs and desires, this question will give you a big advantage over other candidates because you'll offer better reasons for being hired than anyone else.

Whether your interviewer asks you this question explicitly or not, *this is the most important question of your interview!* After all, the interviewer must answer this question favorably in his or her own mind before you'll be hired. So, here's what to do. Walk through each of the position's requirements as you understand them, and follow each with how well you meet that requirement.

EXAMPLE: "As I understand your needs, you are first and foremost looking for someone who can expand your book distribution channels. In my prior position, my innovative promotional ideas doubled, and then tripled, the number of outlets selling our books. I'm confident I could do the same for you. You also need someone to energize your mail-order sales. Here, too, I believe I have exactly the experience you need. Over the last five years, I've increased mail-order sales at Hampshire Advertising from $600,000 to $2,800,000."

Every one of these selling couplets (employer's need matched by your accomplishment stories) is a touchdown that runs up your score. This is your best opportunity to outsell your competition.

What did you like best/least about your last job?

TRAP QUESTION. Never state anything negative! Explain what you liked best. Then say, "While every job has its challenges, I've been fortunate enough to learn and grow professionally in each of the positions I've held."

In your last position, how much of the work did you do on your own, and how much as part of a team? Which did you enjoy more?

Talk in terms of your flexibility and adaptability—your ability to work in whatever mode seems appropriate to the situation. Make it clear that you have been equally effective in teams or working independently, as each case demanded. You enjoy both; it's more about what will work best for the project and the company at that time.

What are some of the more difficult problems you have encountered in your past jobs? How did you solve them?

Tell two or more preprepared accomplishment stories that are related to the company's stated needs and challenges. Keep it positive!

The Hypothetical Problem

Sometimes an interviewer will describe a difficult business situation and ask, "How would you handle this?" Since it's virtually impossible to have all of the facts in front of you at the interview, don't fall into the trap of trying to solve this problem and giving your verdict on the spot. It will make your decision-making process seem woefully inadequate and impulsive.

Instead, describe the rational, methodical process *you would follow* in analyzing this type of problem: generating solutions, choosing the best course of action, and monitoring the results. Remember, whenever responding to such "What would you do?" questions, always describe your thinking process or working methods, along with past successes addressing similar challenges (accomplishment stories). With this approach, you'll never go wrong.

Did you ever make suggestions to senior management? What happened?

Say "yes." Tell some accomplishment stories and results, in which you positively influenced senior management.

At your previous job(s), what did you think management could have done to make you function more effectively as an employee?

TRAP QUESTION. Never state anything negative! Say something like, "My employer was very good in providing resources and support to my position, so I have no complaints about this."

What has kept you from progressing faster and farther in your career?

TRAP QUESTION. Never state anything negative! Say, "I don't know what could have given you the impression that I'm dissatisfied with the progress and pace of my career. I'm quite satisfied with where my career is at this point in my life. However, I am definitely prepared to take on greater challenges and contribute at a higher level."

What else should we know about you?

This is a perfect invitation for you to tell one or two more of your best accomplishment stories. (Are you getting the message that your accomplishment stories are your *best* selling tool?) Then, repeat how well-suited you are for the opportunity and how interested you are in the job.

Tell me about the best/worst boss you've ever had.

TRAP QUESTION: Never state anything negative! Say that while every boss has been different, you've worked productively with, and learned something from, each one. (Be prepared to give some examples of what you've learned.)

Everybody likes to criticize. What do people criticize about you?

TRAP QUESTION. Never state anything negative! Say that you can't think of any criticisms you have received from colleagues on the job. Of course, there have been areas for development, such as when your supervisors would have given you performance reviews, and they might have made some suggestions for improvement. Say that you've always taken these suggestions seriously and have taken steps to make the improvements that were requested. Add that this has made you stronger as a professional. (Give at least one example.)

Everyone has pet peeves. What are yours?

TRAP QUESTION. Never state anything negative! Turn this question around, by talking about your high professional standards. Your only pet peeves are with yourself—pushing yourself hard and not accepting mediocrity, for example—or how you are always striving to reach your full potential on the job, etc.

What is your leadership style?

Talk in terms of your flexibility and adaptability—your ability to lead in whatever mode seems appropriate to the situation. Explain that it's more about what approach will work best for the project and the company at that time. Give an example or two, demonstrating different leadership styles, using your relevant accomplishment stories.

Are you geographically mobile? (or) Are you willing to travel?

Ask for clarification—what exactly does the interviewer mean? Then, according to the degree of travel requirements, either say, "That would be no problem at all," or tell them, "I'd like to give it some thought or discuss it with my family, and get back to you within 24 hours."

You don't have the experience/background for this position. How could you handle it?

Say you're confused by their comment, that you're quite confident that you *do* have the right experience and background for this position, and that you're a very strong match for the responsibilities. Ask what specifically concerns them about your background. (Sometimes the interviewer is just testing you.) Restate your qualifications as needed, tying your accomplishment stories to the employer's requirements.

You're overqualified for this position, aren't you? (even if you are slightly overqualified)

This is often code that translates to the interviewer thinking either "You'll probably ask for too much money" or "You're too old for this job."

Say, "Actually, I see a lot of challenges in this opportunity, and I'm sure that I would find the work extremely interesting." Give some examples of what you mean, and talk about the new dimensions of experience and skill that you would bring to the position, almost as though you would expand the level of contribution in this job, thus making the job much more than it is at present.

We have all the information we need. We'll be in touch.

Take the initiative. Ask such questions as, "Where do I stand? Am I being considered as a strong candidate? When should I expect to hear from you, or would you prefer that I contact you in a day or two? What is your time frame for making a final decision? Is there anything else I can provide to facilitate the process?" Then, confirm your strong interest in the position and restate how confident you are that your background is an ideal match to the job. Be sure to get a follow-up phone call or meeting onto the employer's calendar, to continue the mutual decision-making process.

The most important interview questions might be the ones *you* ask. In the interview, don't think you're the only one who is on the spot. It is perfectly acceptable for you to ask questions of the interviewer and to take notes throughout the meeting (which will help you to formulate your questions). When an interviewer asks, "So, do you have any questions for me?" the *worst* thing you could possibly say is "Nope."

In some cases, you'll be judged more on the *questions* you're asking than the answers you're giving. After all, you might wind up working for this individual, so it's important for you to find out as much as you can about how he or she works, thinks, and communicates. Additionally, asking these types of questions will help you sound like an articulate, savvy business professional. You'll seem well-prepared and genuinely interested in working for the organization.

Take a look at some of these questions that *you can ask* the interviewer, and then feel free to come up with even more of your own:

- Can you give me more detail about the position's responsibilities?
- Where do you see this position going in the next few years?
- What are two or three significant things you would want me to accomplish in my first few months?
- How often has this position been filled in the past two to five years?
- What would you like done differently by the next person who fills this position?

- How can I most quickly become a strong contributor within the organization?
- How will my performance be evaluated, and at what frequency?
- What are the most challenging aspects of the job for which I am being considered?
- How are loyalty and hard work rewarded at this organization?
- How would you define or describe your own management style?
- What are the strengths and weaknesses of my prospective subordinates, as you see them?
- With whom will I be interacting most frequently, and what are their responsibilities? What will be the nature of our interaction?
- What would the limits of my authority and responsibility be?
- What particular things about my background, experience, and style interest you? What makes you think I'll be successful? What causes you concern about my candidacy?
- What freedom would I have to act and what budget would be available to me for: (a) changes in staffing, promotion, salary increases; (b) use of consultants, requesting or purchasing software and hardware systems, capital for new ideas and approaches; (c) changes within my area regarding policies, procedures, practices, performance, and expectations?
- How do you like your people to communicate with you? (verbally, in writing, informally, in meetings, by phone, voicemail, e-mail, only when necessary?)
- What are some of your longer-term objectives?
- Why did you join this company? Why have you stayed?
- Now that we've had a chance to talk, how does my background measure up to the requirements of the job? To the other candidates?
- Am I being seriously considered for this position?
- Where are you in the process? What's our next step?
- If I don't hear from you within (time period), would it be ok to call you?
- Could you take me on a brief tour of the building including the area in which I would be working?

Note: You'll find many more interview questions that *you* can ask in the Career Resources section at the end of this book.

Prepare thoroughly for your interviews by studying and practicing both your answers and your questions.

Did you know that business leaders and political candidates regularly and rigorously practice their press conferences, debates, media interviews, and speeches over and over again in front of a mirror, in a room with their close advisors, with both audio and video recorders, and even alone in the car, in the shower, and anyplace else they can grab a few minutes of focused time?

They practice so much that they start to internalize the natural rhythm and flow of their message. They develop sound bites—key phrases, taglines, and signature stories that they can reel off effortlessly and authentically. You should strive for this level of professionalism and polish in your own interviews. If you do this successfully, there should never be a situation in which you struggle to come up with a response on the spot.

It needs to be said again: I *strongly* recommend that you thoroughly prepare for your interviews by studying and practicing both your answers and your questions. Get someone to help you, by doing a role-play, in which your friend can be the interviewer and you can play the part of the job candidate. Then, you should switch roles.

In addition, some people find working through these questions with an audio recorder to be useful (record your answers and practice until you sound natural, confident, and real). You'll reduce your anxiety, boost your confidence, and perform much better if you know your lines in advance. And remember—*never state anything negative* in a job interview.

Follow-Up Steps after the Interview

My career coaching clients often express frustration after they've completed their interviews for a position they want. The common complaints include, "Why doesn't the company call me back?" or "I feel like I have no power; all I can do is wait for an answer!" or "Can't I do anything to make the employer say yes?" After helping thousands of clients through the interview process, here is what I can tell you: There is no magic bullet that will get the employer to offer you the job. In fact, you're probably already doing most of the right things in this process.

You'll be happy to know, however, that there are some strategies you can use to *influence* the employer's decision and finesse the process. Changing many of your small actions and approaches can actually make a big difference in the outcome of your interviews.

> There are some strategies you can use to influence the employer's decision and finesse the process.

Here are ten suggestions for navigating through the interview process and following up:

1. **Set the stage for effective follow-up.** The first strategy is to have a structured follow-up system in the first place (which most candidates do not). You should have a plan in place *before* you even get to the interview. This way, you'll be able to put the wheels in motion immediately, and you won't have to think about it. This step alone will relieve the pressure and decrease your anxiety. Plus, you'll feel prepared and in control. Developing your follow-up strategy *before* the interview will even enhance your behavior *during* the interview.
2. **Act more like a consultant than an applicant.** When you're at the interview, don't spend all your time trying to sell yourself. Focus instead on asking intelligent, probing questions about the employer's business needs, problems, and challenges (like a good consultant would). These questions should be based on the preparation and study you've done beforehand. Write down the interviewer's answers, which will become the foundation for your follow-up steps. Whenever possible, give specific examples (accomplishment stories) from your work history that are directly relevant to the interviewer's stated issues.
3. **Don't rush toward an offer.** Offers for professional-level jobs are almost *never* made at the first interview. So, don't rush the process! The purpose of your initial interview is not to get an offer, but to get invited back for a second meeting—most likely with a higher-level individual at the company. Use every interview to ask more questions and uncover the employer's primary needs and problems. The more of these challenges you uncover, the better prepared you'll be to submit your Work Proposal at the appropriate time.
4. **Confirm the next steps.** At the end of each meeting, be sure to plan and confirm the next steps. Remember, an interview (or *any* meeting, for that matter) is only as good as the follow-up actions that it generates. Don't settle for "We'll let you know" or similar comments that place you in a passive position. Assume a more active role, and get a commitment from the employer for what comes next.

5. **Follow-up promptly and compellingly.** Now that your interview is over, be sure to send your thank-you letters as soon as possible. These should be personalized to each individual (not generic), and must include specific references to each person with whom you met (something they said or contributed). Be sure your correspondence is as professional and clear as it can be, whether via e-mail or snail mail. If you promised to send the employer additional documents or information, do so promptly.
6. **Use every follow-up contact as a chance to build your value.** After the interview, carefully review your notes that highlight the company's most pressing needs, problems, and challenges. Identify specific areas where you have successfully addressed similar issues in your career. In your thank-you letter, include brief synopses of these accomplishments, tying them directly to the company's stated challenges (usually in a side-by-side chart format). You can even support your claims by sending the employer actual samples of your work. Most companies want employees who are true problem solvers, so this will prove that you have what it takes and that you can bring your special value to the organization.
7. **Be punctual and persistent.** It shouldn't even be necessary to mention this strategy, but some candidates sabotage their chances for the offer by arriving late to the interview or by dropping the ball in the middle of the process. So, always call when you say you're going to call and do what you say you're going to do. Be meticulous in your business etiquette, which includes consistent, regular follow-ups by phone and e-mail.
8. **Leverage outside resources.** If you have contacts and connections with anyone who might influence the hiring decision, or who actually knows the interviewer, ask them to put in a good word for you. But do this advisedly, because it can be a sensitive or highly political matter at times. At the very least, send the employer some letters of recommendation, written by respected professionals in your field or business community.
9. **Accept rejection gracefully.** Assuming you've done everything you can reasonably do to win the offer, you must accept whatever decision the employer makes. If you get the message (directly or indirectly) that the company is not interested in you, or if they actually reject you, then all you can do is move on. You can't force the interviewer to make you an offer, no matter how perfect you may have thought the job was for you.

10. **Turn defeat into victory.** After being rejected, the first thing you should do (ironically) is to send a thank-you letter. You can really distinguish yourself from the other rejected candidates if you send this sort of polite, professional letter after the fact. Express your sincere appreciation for their consideration, and wish the new employee every success. State that you would be happy to be considered for the position again, should the selected candidate not work out for any reason. (You'd be surprised how many times the new hire does not work out.) When the employer needs to find a quick replacement, there will be a high likelihood that *you* will be at the top of their list. In some cases, the employer may even be so impressed with your gracc and profcssionalism that they will offer you a different position at the company as soon as a vacancy occurs. If you genuinely liked the company, stay in touch with them over the long term. Other opportunities will open up, so make it easy for the employer to contact and eventually hire you.

By applying these follow-up strategies after the interview, you'll improve your chances of getting more offers, and you'll also feel more empowered and effective throughout the hiring process.

62. Seal the Deal with Testimonials

After a great interview, you want to cement the positive impact you just made. And, no, a thank-you letter is *not* sufficient to make you stand out from the crowd anymore. You still need to send it, but what else can you send to prompt the next step, whether that might be a follow-up interview or an actual job offer?

Testimonial statements are very powerful, because they reinforce the positive impression you made in person.

Testimonial statements are very powerful, because they reinforce the positive impression you made in person. Testimonials also have a useful psychological effect: they reassure the interviewer(s) that liking you is *not* a mistake or a risk, and that you have a solid track record of accomplishment that is recognized and endorsed by a long line of other executives and decision makers. Testimonials also employ a powerful selling technique, called third-party validation. (Interviewers will always put more weight on what *others* say about you than what *you* say about you).

Testimonials are very easy to compile. Simply take the letters of recommendation you already have, and choose the best, most positive excerpts from each one and combine them into a single page of rave reviews. With testimonials, it's the words that count—not the dates the testimonials were given, not the context of the statements, and not the particular company or industry they came from. Testimonial comments are truly evergreen. The main point is that the testimonials are about you—your personality, skill, capability, track record, and reputation for getting the job done to the betterment of the organizations you've served.

Salespeople, business owners, and consultants use testimonials all the time—and savvy career self-marketers use them, too. Take a look at the examples on the following pages, and then start to compile your own one-pager of testimonial clips to send after an interview—or anytime you need an extra shot of credibility.

63. Negotiation: The Rules of the Game Work in Any Economy

You might think it's crazy to negotiate a job offer when no one's hiring. You might ask, "I should be thrilled to get *any* offer in this economy, shouldn't I?" The answer is, "No, not necessarily." The hard part comes *after* the offer. So you've aced the interview, passed all the screens, sealed the deal with your testimonials, and your prospective employer is convinced that you're the right person for the job. They make you an offer, and now the tough part begins.

"What?" you say. What could be tough about a job offer? Isn't this my ultimate goal? What's so tough about saying, "Yes, I'll take it. Glad to be on board!"

> Getting the job offer is *not* your ultimate goal.

Well, the fact is, that getting the job offer is *not* your ultimate goal. Your real goal throughout this entire process has been *to take charge of your career, find a job you love, and earn what you deserve*. If you simply

Sample: Testimonial Comments #1

Steven Troy

818 Moorestown Road
Portland, OR 90521
acelawyer@msn.com

Cell: 222-555-8888
Home: 555-789-1234

Testimonial Comments

"I want to thank you for all that you have done for the litigation offices. You legitimized our existence and made us feel that we were part of the law department. Thank you for your team building and taking the time to meet with all of us. It is nice to know that we are valuable to the overall organization!"

—Kevin Kerkorian, Staff Litigation Counsel, Bank Street Insurance Companies

"You are the best general counsel that this company has ever had!"

—Allison Barker, Controller, Reno Rubberband Company

"During the eight years I worked with Steven, he was one of the most knowledgeable individuals of both corporate insurance and securities laws. His honesty and ethics in dealing with other members of management were outstanding and all who worked with him valued his opinions and counsel!"

—Raymond Gobbitz, Chief Information Officer, Ringold Advertising Group

"Steven's training and experience are valuable assets to our company, I am confident that he will continue to make many important contributions to the organization!"

—Raymond Cessna, President & CEO, Howard Central Bank

"Congratulations on your promotion to Secretary and General Counsel. I value your expertise very much and enjoy working with you. I am pleased that you have been given this opportunity and I have the utmost faith in your abilities. I look forward to working with you in your new capacity!"

—Brian Musselman, VP, Human Resources, Scallywag Manufacturing Corporation

"I am confident of your ability to perform the role of Secretary and General Counsel and function as a key member of my management team. I welcome the opportunity to work more closely with you in meeting the challenges we face!"

—Sarah Rickey, Purchasing Director, Meeting House Associates, Inc.

"Congratulations on your promotion to Senior Vice-President. It is nice to see your hard work and contributions to the organization rewarded. You have certainly played an integral part in the growth of this company, and you should be proud of your accomplishments!"

—Jim Palmer, Executive Vice President, Horace Insurance Group

"You are a great lawyer!"

—Mort Payne, Vice President, Rooster Apparel Group

Sample: Testimonial Comments #2

Bernard G. Crause

2632 Cypress Street, Millersville, NJ 33669
Home 555-555-6124
bgc5555@lettermail.net

Testimonial Comments

"I highly recommend Mr. Crause for any organization. We found him to be reliable, honest, hardworking and accountable. He demonstrated a commitment to the goals of our organization and gave full support to other members of the staff!"
—D. Garrison, Development Company President

"My staff and I are very impressed with Mr. Crause's professionalism and business knowledge. He is 'all about' getting the job done, and gets right to the point. I have the utmost respect for his abilities, and his organizational planning is of the highest quality. He is an outstanding employee!"
—H. Rennock, Housing Authority Executive Director

"When we realized the schedule was as difficult as the client, we decided Bernie Crause was the only person for the job. His strong commitment, effort, and dedication were the key contributions towards the project's success!"
—J. Robinson, Development Company Vice President

"At all times and without exception, Mr. Crause has proven to be an honest, hardworking, dedicated individual. His decision making and problem solving abilities are exceptional. He also possesses outstanding communication skills, and works extremely well with interdepartmental groups and government agencies!"
—V. Newman, Casino Director

"I recommend Mr. Crause for all aspects of capital projects development. He demonstrated skills in all aspects of planning and construction, including design management, jurisdictional approvals, bid evaluation, code and safety compliance, payment review and approvals, inspections, and final close-out. Mr. Crause's interpersonal skills are outstanding. He can be an assertive negotiator while remaining calm and friendly. He communicates productively with all team-members, from executives to laborers. Bernie Crause has consistently exceeded our expectations!"
—W. Middleton, College Director

say yes to the first offer that comes along, you are doing none of those three things very well.

Even though you may be tempted to accept any offer to get some income flowing again, you don't want to settle for something you'll regret later. The time to negotiate is now. You can't accept whatever the employer offers just to get in the door, and then try to renegotiate later. It's a now-or-never proposition.

In many situations, especially at higher executive levels, one of the very strengths the employer is looking for is *negotiating skill.* If you don't negotiate (and negotiate well) during the job offer process, the employer might start to think that they've made a mistake in offering you the job.

64. Don't Be Afraid to Negotiate in a Down Market—Be Afraid *Not* to

Most people (who are not accustomed to negotiating) are afraid that negotiating will:

- Make them look too pushy or demanding
- Make them seem ungrateful for the job offer in a tight job market
- Tag them as a high-maintenance prima donna, and not a team player
- Make future raises or promotions more difficult to obtain
- Start off the relationship with their manager on a bad note

In reality, your negotiating ability is a strength and an asset to your prospective employer. By negotiating effectively right from the start, you are demonstrating that when you're on the other side of the desk, you'll negotiate on behalf of the company to make the best deals, get the best prices, and generate the most profit. Some hiring managers even go so far as to say that when candidates do no negotiating at all, or stop negotiating too early in the process, they are disappointed.

> Your negotiating ability is a strength and an asset to your prospective employer.

Everyone knows that negotiating for your livelihood is serious business. But in another way, negotiating is a game. The fact is that employers win this game the majority of the time. Want to know why? *Because most job seekers don't know the rules!* It's pretty tough to win a game when you don't know how the game is played, right?

So, in this section, we'll spend some time learning the game. Now remember, it *is* a game. Games have rules. Games are supposed to be fun. And as is true in all games, the more you practice, the better you'll do. Let's lay out the 21 rules of this game, to ensure that you'll be on a level playing field at your next negotiation.

65. Twenty-One Rules of the Negotiating Game (No Matter How Bad the Job Market Is)

1. Do extensive salary research, preparation, and practice beforehand.
2. Defer salary discussions until an offer seems imminent.
3. Discuss salary only with the ultimate decision-maker.
4. Get the employer to state a salary figure or range first.
5. Wait until an actual offer is extended *before* negotiating anything.
6. Discuss salary only after you have fully described your relevant accomplishments.
7. Know your strategy before attending the negotiation meeting.
8. *Always* negotiate the offer, no matter how good it seems initially.
9. Finalize the salary first, before negotiating other items such as benefits.
10. Never misrepresent your former salary.
11. Don't confuse salary with the full compensation package.
12. Avoid tying your potential salary to your old salary.
13. Use silence as one of your most powerful negotiating tools.
14. Fit is more important than financial compensation.
15. Leverage one offer against other offers if possible.
16. Be patient and disciplined throughout the process.
17. You don't get what you deserve; you get what you negotiate.
18. Never accept or reject an offer on the spot—do a thorough analysis.

19. You can only win at negotiation if you're willing to walk away.
20. Be sure the compensation package you finally accept is a win–win.
21. Maintain a positive, upbeat attitude and enjoy the game.

66. The Simplest Formula for Negotiating Success

Here is a very simple formula for negotiation success:

P + P = P

Preparation + Practice = Power. That's *power*, as in, having the ability to get everything you deserve in the negotiation. Just like during the interview process, *preparation* is one of the keys. And you'll also need to *practice* some of the following negotiating tactics before you're fully comfortable with them. If you do these things, you'll be prepared for any negotiation, and you'll play the game to win.

67. Salary Negotiation Made Simple: What to Say and How to Say It

I am often asked by clients, "What do I do when the help-wanted ad or Internet job posting I'm responding to demands that I include my salary history?" Another typical statement is, "I got a call about an interesting opportunity, but they wanted to know right away what salary I was looking for!" As we discussed earlier in the section on recruiters and search firms, you'll need to determine right away if the person is an external recruiter or an internal recruiter (employee of the company). Your strategy will be different depending on the answer.

If it's an external recruiter, you should share your salary expectations. After all, external recruiters have a vested financial interest in getting you the largest possible salary, because most of their compensation comes as a percentage of their successful candidate's salary.

On the other hand, when you're dealing with an internal employee, such as a human resources representative, any premature mention of your compensation requirements or your salary history will only hurt you later, when you're dealing with the ultimate decision maker during your real negotiations.

> You don't have to play by the rules of the employer or recruiter when it comes to discussions about compensation.

Remember, one of our main goals is for you to take charge of your career, and this includes mastering the entire negotiation process. You need to learn how to deflect and defer these up-front questions about compensation. You don't have to play by the rules of the employer or recruiter when it comes to discussions about compensation. The reason most people get into trouble at this juncture is that they simply don't know how to respond. They've never learned what to say or how to say it when they get confronted by these salary questions.

Well, there is a way out of this dilemma. There are specific words, phrases, and behaviors you can use to turn the tide of your compensation discussions, so that you'll be more in charge of the process and produce the negotiation results you really want. Take the time to study all of the following examples, and practice this dialogue *before* you step into any negotiations. If you're like most of my career coaching clients, you'll be *amazed* at the results. And remember, you're learning these negotiation strategies not just to get a better salary in your next job, but also to maximize your compensation for the rest of your working life.

> There are specific words, phrases, and behaviors you can use to turn the tide of your compensation discussions.

How to Handle First-Round Negotiations (*Before* the Offer)

"What Salary Would You Require?" or "What Were You Making at Your Last Job?"

"I think compensation is a very important topic, and I would be more than happy to discuss it once a mutual interest has been established." (Get back to discussing your accomplishments)

Other responses you could use include...

"Your company has a very good reputation, and I'm sure the compensation package will be fair enough to keep me motivated and productive. (By the way, what is the salary range for this position?")

"Based on my accomplishments, I would like to be paid at the same level as other employees of my caliber. (What is the salary range for a person of my caliber?)"

"Regarding compensation, my needs are flexible and negotiable, and I'd be happy to discuss this once a mutual interest has been established." (Get back to discussing your accomplishments)

"If we decide that I'm the right person for this job, I'm sure we'll be able to come to an agreement on compensation." (Get back to discussing your accomplishments)

"At this time, I'm most interested in determining if I am the right candidate for this job. If there's a fit, I'm sure salary won't be an issue." (Get back to discussing your accomplishments)

"Are you making me an offer? (If so, what salary range did you have in mind?)" *Note*: only use this response later in the negotiation process, after several discussions.

How to Handle First-Round Negotiations (*After* the Offer)

When the issue of a specific salary number or range comes up, and the employer states a number or range, do your best to maintain a poker face (no reaction or expression). Write down all the details. You may repeat the offer back to the interviewer, just to be sure you have all the details right. Then ask, "Do I have all the information about the offer now? Is there anything I omitted?"

At this point, you'll want to move into a sort of play-acting role to produce the results you want. One effective technique is to break eye contact with the interviewer—act slightly disappointed and perplexed. You might look down at the floor, exhale audibly and shake your head slightly, while mentally projecting the thought, "This is far less than what I was expecting. How could they offer me such a low amount, after everything I've told them about my qualifications and accomplishments?"

Do not *say* anything. Remain silent until the interviewer responds. Nobody likes silence in a business meeting, so he or she will probably respond after a moment, offering one of these three comments:

1. "You don't seem too happy with our offer; what number did *you* have in mind?"
2. "I might be able to do a little better, but I'll need to discuss it with my manager."
3. "That's the absolute best we can do; I'm sorry."

Of course, the fourth option is that the interviewer could just sit there and remain silent too (for a very long time), in which case you may need to break the ice by saying something like...

"Based on the level of contribution I offer and the commitment that I am prepared to make"—*pause*—"I believe that your offer is on the conservative side."

(OR)

"In view of the accomplishments that I've shared with you and my 15 years of related experience"—*pause*—"Frankly, your offer is not at all what I was expecting."

Note: The important thing is that you have succeeded in getting the employer to state the salary or range first. Now you're ideally positioned to negotiate for a stronger package.

Then you might add a percentage (perhaps 15 to 20 percent), or state the higher dollar figure you have in mind, whichever seems appropriate. Then *just wait* again, in silence. As I hope you have learned by now, silence is one of your most powerful negotiation tactics!

> Silence is one of your most powerful negotiation tactics.

How to Handle Second-Round Negotiations

Never accept or reject an offer on the spot—ask for 24 hours to one week (depending on the position and the employer's situation) to consider the offer.

Meet again (in person, if possible) with the hiring manager (not Human Resources), and say:

"This is a great opportunity and I'm very excited about working with you (or) joining your company. I am *inclined* to accept your offer, *however* there are three (or more) items I want to discuss (negotiate) with you. If we can reach agreement on these items, I'll be prepared to accept your offer today." (Of course, you should use this approach *only* if you are serious about accepting their offer, if they can meet your terms.)

In your own mind, you may really only need the employer to enhance the offer in two categories (say, salary and vacation days)—but you should ask for improvements in three or four areas (you could also ask for a better bonus or a laptop computer, for example). Always ask for more than what you really want, because in most cases you won't get everything you ask for. Then, you'll be able to settle for what you actually wanted in the first place.

> Always ask for more than what you really want, because in most cases you won't get everything you ask for.

Know Exactly What You Need and Exactly What You Want

Savvy negotiators have two sets of criteria for evaluating offers. They know:

- What they *need* to accept an offer (bottom-line minimum, or they walk away)
- What they *want* in an ideal offer (for the perfect deal)

You also need to look at all the dimensions of your ideal job and ideal employer. You should review what your bare minimum acceptable terms would be, and also review what perfect would mean to you. The exercises and work you did early on in this book should come in very handy here.

Sample: Need/Want Chart (Downloadable)

Need	Want
$60,000 Base	$75,000 Base
2 Weeks Vacation	4 Weeks Vacation
Benefits Start in 3 Months	Benefits Start Now
Management Role	Director Title
Transportation Expenses	Company Car
Adequate Workspace	Private Office
Severance Pay	Outplacement Support
Bonus Eligible	Stock Plan

To download this element of your Job Search Survival Toolkit, visit: www.CareerPotential.com/bookbonus.

After you make your own need/want chart, think about what you're willing to trade and what you're not. Make your own list.

68. Everything Is Negotiable—Yes, *Everything*

Sometimes, people get into a locked mindset about negotiating, with all sorts of assumptions, preconceived notions, and myths. This is even more true in tough economic times, when no one's hiring. The truth is that *everything* is *always* negotiable.

> The truth is that *everything* is *always* negotiable.

Let's review how negotiating works from the other side of the desk. There are four things I guarantee you, from all my years of experience in career coaching:

1. The first salary offer the employer makes is the *lowest* offer they can possibly utter without feeling completely embarrassed.
2. The employer is fully expecting you to negotiate, and will think twice about making you an offer if you don't know how to play the game of negotiation.
3. About 80 percent of the outcome of your negotiation will be determined by your attitude and assumptions.
4. You *can* learn to negotiate compensation effectively. You just need to learn a specific set of behaviors and phrases.

> The first salary offer the employer makes is the *lowest* offer they can possibly utter without feeling completely embarrassed.

Let's outline all the items you might consider negotiating for:

- Salary (always finalize this first)
- Job title
- Job responsibilities
- Insurance (life, medical, dental, disability)
- Vacation time
- Office location

- Retirement plans
- Relocation assistance
- Training/professional development allowances
- Workspace
- Bonuses (sign-on and performance)
- Commission rates
- Expense accounts
- Memberships and dues
- Accelerated performance/salary reviews
- Stock options
- Profit sharing
- Company car or auto allowance
- Home purchase or mortgage assistance
- Tuition reimbursement
- Noncompete agreements
- Outplacement/career transition assistance
- Consultant vs. employee status
- Flex-time
- Telecommuting
- Job sharing
- Free lunches (other meals)
- Company-sponsored child care
- Severance settlement package
- Legal, tax, or financial advice
- Discount on purchases
- Computer equipment
- Health club membership
- Paid company services (cell phone service, air travel, etc.)
- And whatever else is important to *you*

Establish the Real Value of an Offer

We indicated earlier that you should always assume that the compensation you're initially offered will be too low and that you should always try to negotiate the numbers *up*. However, to be fair, you should also give consideration to the full scope of the compensation package. Be sure to *get the whole story* before you judge the compensation. There may be more to the offer than meets the eye. Don't forget to factor in the dollars *other than* the salary itself that go into a compensation offer.

Take a look at this sample compensation worksheet:

Sample: Real Value of an Offer Form (Downloadable)

- Base Salary	$50,000
- Health Plan }	
- Vacation }	(35%)
- Retirement Plan }	$17,500
- Training & Development	
- Auto Allowance	
- Bonus }	(15%)
- Commission }	$7,500
- Etc.	
TOTAL COMP	**$75,000**

To download this element of your Job Search Survival Toolkit, visit: www.CareerPotential.com/bookbonus.

69. The Number-One Most Important Salary Negotiating Fact

I'm going to have to draw you a picture of this point and burn it into your long-term memory—it's *that* important:

That's right. There is no connection between your old salary and your new salary. Your old salary is based on the past—different job, different company, different circumstance, different experience level, different time, different product, different *everything*.

> There is *no* connection between your old salary and your new salary.

Of course, employers will try to use salary as a screening mechanism, but that doesn't mean you have to let them. Don't let the prospective employer tie your new salary (currently under negotiation) to your old salary in any way, shape, or form. Each time this happens, you, the candidate, will lose. And the sad thing is that this unfortunate situation is completely preventable.

Look Beyond the Money

When you're deep into negotiations, and you're doing well, remember to ask the big question: *Is this the right fit?* The fit of a job is of paramount importance, even in a terrible job market. Think again about all the factors that brought you this far. Does everything fit—your background, personality, strengths, interests, passions, and capabilities? Will you enjoy working at this job in six weeks, six months, six years? Think about such factors as:

- Compensation
- Location
- Industry
- Product or service
- Headquarters or remote
- Size or revenues
- Reputation or prestige
- Pace
- Formal or informal
- People and relationships
- Physical environment
- Culture
- Values and mission

> The fit of a job is of paramount importance, even in a terrible job market.

Let's be realistic. When no one's hiring, there may be a measure of compromise to a job you accept—and that's perfectly fine. But you must know your own priorities. Just because an offer has been made, and you're putting on your best game in the negotiation process, does *not* mean that this is necessarily the right job. Be flexible, but don't lose sight of the big-picture goals that you've worked so hard to identify.

Sometimes, the toughest negotiating we need to do is with ourselves. But if you've done your homework, thought about your priorities, and have a clear sense of what you want, you'll be able to make a solid decision that will benefit both your career and your employer in the long run.

70. Comparing, Accepting, and Rejecting Offers

Yes, it's true. There may come a time when you'll have multiple offers on the table at the same time, and *you*—not the employer—will decide where you will work.

> YOU—not the employer—will decide where you will work.

If you've done everything up to this point the way it needs to be done, the principle of "when it rains, it pours" will come into play. In fact, it happens more often than you might expect (to the shock and surprise of my career coaching clients). It's important to be ready to make a clear-cut, apples-to-apples comparison of the different offers as they come in. You may even conduct parallel negotiation sessions, to arrive at the best competing offers you possibly can. The easiest way to do this is to take an objective look at each of the offers, and map out how they compare. What follows is a sample form that will help you do exactly that.

While we're on the subject of receiving job offers and accepting or rejecting them, let me also provide some sample cover letters that should come in handy at this stage of your search process.

Sample: Job Offers Comparison Form (Downloadable)

	Rank from 1 (low) to 10 (high)		
	Offer #1	**Offer #2**	**Offer #3**
Career/Professional Criteria			
Job satisfaction			
Scope of responsibilities			
Do work at which I am skilled			
Title			
Professional growth			
Expand my competencies			
Take on higher level challenges			
Get promoted			
Workspace/office environment			
Manage others			
Other			
Company Criteria			
Company size			
Management style			
Image and reputation of company			
Quality of technology			
Adequacy of staff and support personnel			
Company culture			
Other			
Personal Criteria			
Base salary			
Bonus, profit-sharing, stock options, etc.			
Benefits (health plan, vacation, 401k, etc.)			
Office location			
Travel requirements and commuting			
Perqs (trips, car, memberships, etc.)			
Special expenses (gas, taxes, relocation, etc.)			
Community, schools, etc.			
Other			
Total Scores			

To download this element of your Job Search Survival Toolkit, visit: www.CareerPotential.com/bookbonus.

Sample: Acceptance Letter (Downloadable)

March 3, 2009

Mr. David Hassel
Director, Office Automation
ZeroGrafix Corporation
55 West 14th Street, Suite J
New York, NY 10011

Dear Mr. Hassel:

I am pleased to accept the position of Information Technology Coordinator, as we discussed last week. The following is my understanding of our mutual agreement:

- Start date will be Monday, April 1, 2009.
- Salary will be $73,500 per year, for a 35-hour workweek.
- I am entitled to two weeks of vacation, which will be increased to three weeks after one year of service.
- I will have a performance review in 6 months, at which time an assessment will be made regarding promotion to Assistant Director of Office Automation, as well as a potential salary increase.

Please call me at 777-555-5555 if you wish to discuss any of the above arrangements. I am excited about this opportunity, and I look forward to a mutually rewarding business relationship.

Thank you again for your confidence in me.

Sincerely,

Georgette Baker

Sample: Turn-Down Letter

March 3, 2009

Mr. David Hassel
Director, Office Automation
ZeroGrafix Corporation
55 West 14th Street, Suite J
New York, NY 10011

Dear Mr. Hassel:

I appreciate the time you took to interview me for the position of Information Technology Coordinator. I was impressed with the efficiency of your operation and the friendliness of your staff.

As I mentioned on the phone the other day, I have determined that this position does not match my skills or salary requirements, so I must reluctantly turn it down. I hope you'll keep me in mind if other positions become available involving more responsibility and greater opportunities to contribute my leadership skills.

Thank you again for meeting with me.

Sincerely,
Georgette Baker

71. Congratulations! You Got the Job (Even When No One Was Hiring)

When you're accepting a job offer, or expect to get an offer, contact the other hot companies on your active Target List that you've met with and let them know you're about to accept another offer.

This does several things for you:

1. It leverages the other employers' fear of loss, which might prompt them to make you an offer if you're already one of their top candidates.
2. It sends a clear message that you're an in-demand asset, and thus may precipitate a hiring decision in your favor.
3. It establishes a competitive environment between two or more potential employers, and gives you an edge in negotiating with either—or both—companies.

The language for this conversation is straightforward and simple. You could say something like, "It looks like I'll be taking a position at. . ." or "As much as I'd like to work with your organization, I need to let you know I have an offer in hand from. . ." (Of course, you should *only* use this strategy if you really do have another job offer in hand.) Once you've established this groundwork, you can see where the employer takes the discussion next. No matter what the final outcome, this strategy can never hurt you if you use it ethically and honestly.

PART V

Bulletproof Your Career, Once and for All

72. Landing Your Job Is Not the End—It's the Beginning

Let's assume that, with the help of this book, you got the job you wanted. Whew, I'll bet you're glad that's over. Now you can relax, coast a while, and rest on your laurels. Right? *Wrong!* The fact is, your work is just beginning, but so is your glory. There are many career challenges still ahead, such as:

- Assimilating into your new position
- Aligning with new company's culture and business priorities
- Developing habits of Perpetual Career Management, which include:
  - Establishing professional credibility and developing productive relationships
  - Avoiding blind spots, leveraging assets, and planning steps toward advancement
  - Continuing to work with your career coach (if you have one) as your partner in career success

> When you land a new job, your work is just beginning, but so is your glory.

73. Celebrate Your New Job

Landing your new job is certainly a wonderful cause for celebration. In fact, *don't forget to celebrate,* because you definitely deserve to after all your hard work! Here's one word of caution: you don't really have the job offer until it's an official, written offer. So, don't tell all your friends about your new job or go out and buy a new car—at least, not yet. Wait until the deal is signed, sealed, and delivered.

After the celebration, write letters or cards to your entire network of active contacts, letting them know about your new position and thanking them for their help. In turn, you should offer *them* help or guidance in a similar capacity, should they ever need it (and they will, eventually).

74. How to Avoid Winding Up on the Street Again

The first several weeks in a new job are usually both exciting and filled with a certain amount of anxiety. Your new tasks and responsibilities are stimulating and perhaps a bit overwhelming. You may be used to being the top dog or expert, and now you're the new kid on the block. Or, you may suddenly be the guy or gal who knows the *least* about some new technology, procedure, or "the way we do things around here." Your new relationships and the unfamiliar corporate environment may also be sources of apprehension as you figure out how to best handle your new role.

During your career transition process, you've learned a lot about yourself—your strengths, your preferences, and how you're wired. You've put in the hours and successfully hired your new employer. Well, the good news is that now is the time and here is the place to maximize the impact of your self-discovery process. Make all those elements you've identified work in your favor. Your new job is a means for you to further develop the key strengths identified in your career assessment work. These are the building blocks of your career.

Start by understanding what your boss's priorities are and what the expectations are for your new position—and for *your* performance, specifically. But before you rush to meet these priorities and expectations, be sure that you also understand the organization's culture, style, and way of doing things.

Your new job is a means for you to further develop the key strengths identified in your career assessment work. These are the building blocks of your career.

75. Perpetual Career Management Is Your Insurance Policy

Beware of a common trap: putting all your time and energy into just doing your job, as compared to managing your career. As we said earlier, your focus should not just be on the job, but on managing your career effectively over the long term. That means *forever,* for as long as you have a career. Let's face it, this sort of downturn in the economy has happened before, and it will certainly happen again. So you'll want to be prepared and positioned for success, no matter what outside circumstances may be.

By turning your attention now to Perpetual Career Management, you'll be maintaining your momentum, ensuring that your career success will endure, and opening a pathway to much higher levels of recognition and achievement. Sure, you'll want to work extra hard to hold onto your job when jobs are scarce, but never forget to also focus on the larger context of your overall career.

Beware of a common trap: putting all your time and energy into just doing your job, as compared to managing your career.

It's no surprise that people who are in career transition focus a lot of their time and energy on updating their resumes, networking, brushing up their interviewing skills, collecting accomplishment stories, and so forth. They know they need to be prepared, to be at the top of their game, if they hope to land another good position.

But what about those of us who are currently working, in jobs that may seem stable even in a bad employment market? If you're like most people, these activities get little or no attention—that is, until you get laid off, fired, or simply become unhappy enough to make a change. It's human nature to become "career complacent" when you have a steady job, focusing all your energy on doing a good job. But when no one's hiring, this approach just won't cut it.

What does this mean for *you*? It means that you should consider adopting a different approach, which I call Perpetual Career Management. Instead of being focused completely on your job, you should be focused on managing your career—at all times, regardless of your work circumstances. Keep thinking of the job as a subset, or as one component of your entire career. In practical terms, Perpetual Career Management means engaging continually in a host of activities that you thought were necessary only for job seekers. Why should you do this? So you'll always be prepared, no matter what happens in your company or your job. Take the current economic climate as an example; it has been quite a wake-up call. By maintaining your focus on career management, if something happens to your job again, you won't be caught flat-footed. Instead of feeling devastated, stuck, or powerless, you'll always have career choices and a sense of control.

To become a Perpetual Career Manager, here are 10 things you should *always* be doing, regardless of your employment situation:

1. **Keep all of your success documents up-to-date.** Resume, list of professional references, letters of recommendation, accomplishment stories, etc. By keeping these documents in a current file, you'll be ready to leverage them at any point of transition (reviews, promotions, job changes), whether these events are planned or unplanned.
2. **Put time aside every week for active networking** to maintain established relationships and develop new ones, both inside and outside of the company where you work. You should always be positioned to leverage your professional and personal contacts when the need arises.
3. **Join and take leadership roles** in appropriate associations and trade organizations. This will boost your visibility and enhance your credibility in your industry.
4. **Write articles or do presentations** focused on your area of expertise in any venue (clubs, conferences, publications, etc.). This type of exposure demonstrates your level of trade skill and expertise—and people will take notice.
5. **Continue your career education** and maintain your industry credentials through seminars, academic classes, lectures, professional events, conferences, new certifications/degrees, and the like. No one wants to hire someone whose knowledge base and trade skills aren't current.
6. **Research and be aware of the competition**, including information about other companies and other professionals in your industry. Always know who they are and what they're doing. Endeavor to know the competition better than they know themselves.
7. **Offer to help people in your network**, even though they may not be in a position to help you back at this time. These people will

remember your good will, and as they say, "What goes around comes around." So, go the extra mile!

8. **Look at new jobs and investigate other opportunities**, even if you're not job hunting at this time. This will help you to know the market, gauge various aspects of your current position, and stay plugged in.
9. **Always ask yourself, "How can I contribute more?"** Doing a good job isn't good enough. The people who land the best jobs and move up in the organization are the ones who clearly demonstrate their value to the organization in measurable ways—every day, every week, every month.
10. **Practice your interviewing, negotiating, and related skills** on a regular basis. Don't wait until another career crisis arises to polish your job seeking skills. You never know what's going to happen. As today's employment picture has shown us, while you can expect the best at work, you should be prepared for the worst.

> The people who land the best jobs and move up in the organization are the ones who clearly demonstrate their value to the organization in measurable ways.

Remember: Never be satisfied or complacent, and don't ever assume you're 100 percent safe in any job. The only real job security is in developing and maintaining your knowledge and competitiveness in the marketplace. By adopting the Perpetual Career Management strategies outlined here, and implementing these behaviors consistently, you'll always be in top form and have plenty of professional options, no matter how low the economy plunges and regardless of how bad the job market gets.

76. Learn from the Past, Build Toward the Future

As we said earlier, it's critically important to demonstrate value and deliver tangible results. You can increase your value to a new employer and improve your chances of success by answering the following questions:

- What skill areas can you improve upon in your next job?
- What do you need to learn in order to work more successfully?

- If you were previously laid off or downsized, what could you do differently to make yourself indispensable in *this* job? Acquire new skills? Develop a better attitude? Take on extra work? Show more initiative?
- How will you keep close tabs on the trends in your industry and your field?
- Do you know where you want to be in one year, three years, and five years?
- What can you do *now* to help you ultimately reach these career goals?

Do your own analysis, listing your lessons learned from the past and outlining new career approaches and initiatives that you'd like to implement moving forward.

77. The First 90 Days Make All the Difference

Some experts believe you have just 90 days in a new job to make your impact and create the *permanent* impression that people in the organization will have of you and your leadership capabilities. You'll either cut it or not—in terms of garnering respect, visibility, and credibility in your new position. The precedents you establish in the first 90 days will last for your entire tenure at the organization, so this trial period is critically important to your long-term success.

Research shows us that approximately 35 to 40 percent of new hires fail within the first 12 to 18 months in their new jobs. Why? Because most focus all of their time and attention on doing the job that they were hired to do. They put their heads down and get busy, believing that if they just do a good job, their positions will be secure. Unfortunately, this approach ends in disaster far too often—with the new employee being dismissed.

> What really distinguishes new hires is how well they assimilate into the company's culture, environment, and key relationships.

Of course, every new employee needs to do a good job in the position for which he or she was hired, but that's just the baseline expectation. What really distinguishes new hires is how well they assimilate into the company's culture, environment, and key relationships. In addition to doing a good job, it's vitally important that you ramp up into your new role with your eyes wide open. This means paying close attention to what's going on all around you, creating the right impressions, attending to interpersonal dynamics, and establishing the right precedents.

78. Relationships Keep You Moving Up in a Down Economy

Establish positive relationships with your new colleagues and develop good communication habits to maintain those relationships. Be honest, open, friendly, reliable, and clear. Pay close attention to the company's internal politics and culture, and align yourself in the most productive ways possible.

Cultivate good relationships with *everyone*, including the employees above and below your level at the organization. Get to know people's names. Reach out to the mail guy, the security guard, the IT guru, your manager's executive assistant—everyone! You want friends in a 360-degree arc around you. Why? Simple—it makes working with these folks a lot more pleasant and productive. And when it's time for another round of layoffs, having good friends at the company could help you avoid getting another pink slip.

79. Establish a Reputation for Producing Tangible Results

Develop a reputation for producing tangible results and for keeping commitments. Immediately start a success file, where you'll record your accomplishments and contributions. Keep track of the positive feedback you get from others—in meetings and in writing from clients, managers, and other departments. Always strive to contribute more, and try to become known as the go-to person. Learn how to dig below the surface. Ask probing questions to discover the problems beneath the problems. This strategy will get you to the core issues, and you'll therefore seem like a hero when you develop the best solutions and generate the strongest results.

80. Communicate, Communicate, Communicate—Then Deliver the Goods

Communicate plans, progress, and results to your superiors and to your team on a consistent basis. Don't keep colleagues in the dark. Develop clear goals and complete projects on time and on budget, while leveraging the cooperation of your team and keeping everyone informed.

Learn to communicate with colleagues (especially supervisors) in ways that work for *them*. Factors to consider include the means of communication (e-mail, phone, face-to-face), the frequency of communication (once a day, every hour, only when asked), and the length or detail of communication (single-sentence e-mails, five-minute meetings, full-hour phone conferences).

> Develop clear goals and complete projects on time and on budget, while leveraging the cooperation of your team and keeping everyone informed of your progress.

If you're not clear about the communication preferences of your boss and coworkers, *ask*. You'll be glad you did, and you'll set the stage for enjoyable relationships in which you'll be most effective.

81. Review and Fine-Tune Your Job Description with Your Manager

In addition to reviewing and revising your job description, make sure to also sit down during those first 90 days and create an Individual Development Plan for yourself and your role. This includes your short-, mid-, and long-term goals at the company. This is critical to make sure that the *job you landed* becomes the *job you love*. This strategy also ensures that you'll be focused on your boss's priorities (alignment), which can also extend your tenure at the company.

Remember that employment is a two-way contract. Your responsibility is to do the best job you possibly can and to help the company achieve its business objectives. The employer's duty is to provide an environment where you can advance your career, pursue new challenges, and develop toward your professional goals. Many companies tend to forget their part of the bargain, so it's up to you to remind them, especially during your first few months on the job.

> Many companies tend to forget their part of the bargain, so it's up to you to remind them.

82. Maintain a Healthy Balance Between Your Work and Private Life

Make sure that you don't go overboard with your enthusiasm for your new job. Family time, hobbies, and recharging your batteries are all part of your long-term professional effectiveness and success. In today's hyperconnected world, it's easy to get obsessed with work. There is strong a temptation to respond to e-mails and cell phone calls 24/7, and to constantly be thinking about the job. Many believe that this work style makes them more efficient, but research clearly shows that this is not the case. If you're constantly distracted and overwhelmed with work, or if you're always worried about keeping your job, you certainly won't be very productive.

Should you work hard when you're at work? Should you put in extra hours when necessary? Should your job be one of the priorities in your life? Absolutely! But the most productive employees are those who establish reasonable boundaries with work and who have satisfying personal lives apart from the job. One way to ensure that your employer will realize the greatest return-on-investment on *you* is to maintain a healthy balance between your personal life and work life. This will make you more productive and will, in turn, increase the likelihood that your company will keep you around for a long, long time.

> One way to ensure that your employer will realize the greatest return-on-investment on *you* is to maintain a healthy balance between your personal life and work life.

83. Never Feel Helpless Again—No Matter How Bad the Job Market Gets

As you can now see, you *do* have a lot more control over your employment situation than you might have thought, even when no one's hiring. No matter how bad the news gets about the job market, there are people just like you landing good jobs every day.

Everything you've learned in this book will help you not only in your current job search, but at every turn in your career, for the rest of your professional life. Through good times and bad, through economic booms and employment crises, you'll never feel helpless again.

By adopting and implementing the powerful career strategies and job search tactics in this book, you are now permanently equipped to take charge of your career, find a job you love, and earn what you deserve. You'll never feel helpless again.

I wish you the best of success in your journey!

What you'll find below is even *more* information for you to use as you continue your career development process. I've provided some great resources and web sites—plus additional tips, interview questions, and job search ideas that I've shared with thousands of people through my seminars, articles, and career coaching work. Don't forget to take advantage of all the downloads available to you at www.CareerPotential.com/bookbonus. I'm sure you'll get a lot out of these tools.

When no one's hiring, resources like these become more important than ever, because you need every last bit of market intelligence, competitive research, salary data, and overall business smarts.

Enjoy!

Thirty-Seven Strategies, Tips, Ideas, and Reminders for When No One's Hiring

1. Stay busy, get active, and be productive.
2. Maintain your momentum.
3. Hire a career coach, or get some sort of consistent career support.
4. If you are struggling emotionally, get counseling help.
5. Read career books and/or attend career seminars.
6. Leverage technology web sites and online services/products.
7. Leverage technology—create career web sites like VisualCV and LinkedIn.
8. Leverage technology—keep in touch with more people more often through social media web sites such as LinkedIn (www.linkedin.com), MySpace (www.myspace.com), Twitter (www.twitter.com), and Facebook (www.facebook.com)—and by using blogs, e-newsletters, and so forth.
9. Differentiate yourself—focus your entire message on tangible results.
10. Differentiate yourself—position yourself as an expert by writing articles and giving presentations.
11. Use the time off wisely—gain more education and expertise through classes, seminars, certifications, professional conferences, degrees, etc.

12. Build and leverage your network, one person at a time.
13. Take a temporary or part-time job.
14. Get out of the house and away from the computer.
15. Do consulting or contract assignments.
16. Build, improve, and enhance your career portfolio (documents, tools, etc.).
17. Do volunteer or pro bono work.
18. Do an internship or apprenticeship.
19. Take care of your health, eat well, exercise, and get enough rest.
20. Don't hide; stay in close touch with friends and family.
21. Maintain your interests and involvement in hobbies.
22. Be more flexible geographically.
23. Structure your job search time and activities, as though it were a real job.
24. Consider shifting industries or roles, if appropriate.
25. Create a job opportunity or combine several roles into one.
26. Put together or join a group of other job seekers, and keep each other accountable.
27. Focus *not* on getting a job but on adding tangible value.
28. Look for a *need,* not for an opening (Work Proposal).
29. Practice interviewing and negotiation skills.
30. Offer to help people in your network, including other job seekers.
31. Get involved, be visible and active in professional organizations.
32. Stay focused on your priorities and goals, and don't settle.
33. Remain confident.
34. Teach a course.
35. Maintain an upbeat, positive attitude (even when it's difficult to do so).
36. Take advantage of the fact that many other job seekers are sitting on the sidelines.
37. Do some work "on spec" to show employers the quality of your work.

List of Great Web Sites to Assist in Your Job Search (Available Online)

This is just a small sampling of all the wonderful Web-based resources that are available to job seekers and career changers. The list changes constantly, but these links should get you started.

Senior Executive Opportunities, $100,000 Plus

www.6figurejobs.com
www.executiveregistry.com
www.execunet.com
www.theladders.com
www.careerjournal.com
www.financialjobnet.com
www.cfo.com
www.netshare.com
www.cio.com
www.ritesite.com

General Career Opportunities

www.worktree.com
www.alljobsearch.com
www.acinet.org
www.monster.com
www.hotjobs.yahoo.com
www.careerbuilder.com
www.getthatgig.com
www.beyond.com/network
www.jobcentral.com
www.jobcircle.com
www.jobbankusa.com
www.careersearch.com
www.jobsniper.com
www.jobvertise.com
www.thingamajob.com
www.vault.com
www.indeed.com

General Career Support

www.quintcareers.com
www.allbusiness.com
www.managementhelp.org

(*Continued on page 186*)

Weekly Job Search Activity Form

The Weekly Job Search Activity Form is a time management and activity measurement tool that is designed to focus your work, keep you on track, and increase your momentum.

Looking at your progress on this form will show exactly where you stand on each of the critical job search behaviors, and allow you to continually improve your productivity from week to week. The more concentrated hours you put in each day and each week, the faster you will reach your career goal.

Below, you'll find a list of the activities you should be tracking and recording on this form, along with definitions of each one. At the end of each day and each week, add up your totals in hours. Feel free to make photocopies of this form, to log all of your job search activities.

Research—Information gathering on industries and companies, done on the Web, at the library, from databases, the business section of newspapers and magazines, local publications, specific employer web sites, annual reports, and press releases

Career Development—Attending industry seminars, job search workshops, meetings with your career coach, continuing education classes, and pursuing certifications and accreditations

One-on-One Networking—Meetings with new contacts, former colleagues, professional friends, centers of influence, connectors, and referral sources—often over coffee or a meal, or at the other person's office

Group Networking—Business card exchanges, chamber of commerce events, trade association meetings, professional conferences, networking clubs, job seeker mixers, and job fairs

Responses to Ads/Postings—Research, filter, and select a small number of online and offline classified or "help wanted" advertisements to respond to each week

Letters/E-mails—All outgoing correspondence via e-mail or "snail mail," excluding responses to job search ads and postings

Contact with Recruiters—Phone and in-person contact with executive recruiters, search firms, and employment agencies

Contact with Employers—Phone and in-person contact with targeted employers, including hiring managers, other decision-makers, and human resources

Job Interviews—Meetings and phone calls to discuss open positions for which you are an active candidate, including individual and group interviews

Job Offers—Meetings and phone calls to receive actual job offers, including negotiating and finalizing all the details

Administration—Buying office supplies, organizing work space, making folders, setting up databases, putting away papers, and following up on project details

Sample: Weekly Job Search Activity Form (Downloadable)

WEEK OF: ____________________

	Mon	Tue	Wed	Thu	Fri	Sat	Sun	**Weekly Totals** (in Hours)
Research								
Career Development								
One-on-One Networking								
Group Networking								
Responses to Ads/ Postings								
Letters/E-mails								
Contact with Recruiters								
Contact with Employers								
Job Interviews								
Job Offers								
Administration								
Daily Totals (in Hours)								**Grand Total** (in Hours)

Comments/Notes for Improvement

To download this element of your Job Search Survival Toolkit, visit: www.CareerPotential.com/bookbonus.

(*General Career Support, Continued*)

www.bls.gov/oco
www.erieri.com
www.salary.com
www.hoovers.com/free
www.employmentspot.com
www.dnb.com/us
www.corporateinformation.com
www.managementcourses.com
www.about.com/careers

List of Web Sites with Useful Career Articles

This tactic will differentiate you from other candidates after a networking meeting or a formal interview: send relevant articles, web links, and news items of value on issues relevant to your contact's business or industry.

This makes you more of a *peer* and certainly more of a *professional* in the eyes of your contact. Simply forward an article or link with a short note, saying something like, "Sally, I came across this article after our meeting and wanted to be sure you saw it. It's very interesting and relevant to our discussion."

But where are you supposed to get this flood of wonderful and useful information? From your own research, of course! For an ongoing stream of news and business information, visit these web sites frequently to mine them for gems to use in your clip file. There are thousands more, of course. So, continue doing your own research.

www.bizjournals.com
http://nytimes.com/pages/business
www.usatoday.com/money/front.htm
www.forbes.com/business
www.money.cnn.com
www.findarticles.com
www.mywire.com
web site of your industry group or trade association(s)
web site of your local newspaper

For an updated and more complete list of web resources and tools, visit www.CareerPotential.com/bookbonus.

Forty-Two More Smart Questions to Ask at the Interview

Often, an interview will end with the interviewer asking if you have any questions about the position, the company, and so forth. As you read earlier in this book, the *worst* response you can give is to say "No." Here is another chance to separate yourself from the crowd and ask some great questions.

There are plenty of books and articles that describe how you should *answer* questions at an interview; here's a list of questions that you can *ask* at the interview. Remember, a successful interview should be more of a balanced dialogue than an interrogation.

Some of these questions may seem bold to you, and some will not be appropriate, depending on the specific situation. You'll probably want to select a handful of the questions listed, and use them at your next interview. The key is to always be well-prepared before any face-to-face meeting.

> A successful interview should be more of a balanced dialogue than an interrogation.

The kind of question that will damage your credibility immediately is the one that shows your lack of preparation, knowledge, or research about the company and their needs. So, always do your homework!

1. What do you really want to see as the outcome of hiring someone into this position?
2. If you could wave a magic wand and create the perfect candidate, how would she and I be different? What would we have in common?
3. What's on the front burner with this position? How would I spend my first 30 days here?
4. What's going best for your company right now? How does this position/department tie into that?
5. What's your dream for this organization?
6. In an ideal world, what would you like to see happen after hiring someone like me?
7. What's the best thing that has happened to the company in the past year?

8. What's the worst thing that has happened to the company in the past year?
9. Tell me a bit more about your own background and work history.
10. How do you define an ideal employee relationship?
11. Who do you consider your best employee at this level and why?
12. What two or three problems, if solved, would make a huge difference?
13. What's most important to your boss?
14. What's most important to your team?
15. What's most important to the CEO on a personal level?
16. Who would be impacted by this hiring decision, whom I have not yet met?
17. How do decisions get made at this company?
18. What drives you crazy?
19. What does your competition envy about your organization?
20. Which competitor do you worry about most?
21. What have you learned from that competitor?
22. What would make you look like a hero after this hiring process is over?
23. What gets you juiced?
24. What business books do you like?
25. Why did you decide to meet with me?
26. When does it get crazy around here? What happens, exactly?
27. Who are your best customers or clients?
28. What else should I know about your organization?
29. How can I add value in my first week here? First month? First year?
30. What would I need to do so that 12 months from now, you'd look back on hiring me as the best hiring decision you've made in a long time?
31. If we started with a clean slate, what would you like to get done?
32. How would you describe yourself?
33. What are you known for? Personally? As a department? As a company?
34. Is there anything off-limits in today's conversation? If so, why?
35. What business magazines do you read?

36. What are your favorite web sites for business?
37. Who else in your organization should I know?
38. What, for you, is the bottom line?
39. What can *I* do for *you*?
40. What would *kill* an applicant for this position? Why?
41. What would *lock in* an applicant for this position? Why?
42. Is there something I should have asked you, but didn't?

The kind of question that will damage your credibility immediately is the one that shows your lack of preparation, knowledge, or research about the company and its needs.

Words to Work by...

No man is born into the world whose work is not born with him.
—James Russell Lowell

The biggest mistake that you can make is to believe that you are working for somebody else. Job security is gone. The driving force of a career must come from the individual. Remember: jobs are owned by the company; you own your career!
—Earl Nightingale

Three things are needed for people to be happy in their work: they must be fit for it, must not do too much of it, and must have a sense of success in it.
—John Ruskin

Work can provide the opportunity for spiritual and personal as well as financial growth. If it doesn't, we are wasting far too much of our lives on it!
—James Autry

Inherently, each of us has the substance within to achieve whatever our goals and dreams define. What is missing is the training, education, knowledge and insight to utilize what we already have.
—Mark Twain

I have learned that success is to be measured not so much by the position one has reached in life, as by the obstacles which one has overcome while trying to succeed.
—Booker T. Washington

People don't succeed by migrating to a "hot" industry or by adopting a particular career-guiding mantra. They thrive by focusing on the question of who they really are, and connecting that to the work they truly love. The choice isn't about a career search so much as an identity quest.
—Po Bronson

Choose a job you love, and you will never have to work a day in your life.
—Confucius

The first essential in a boy's career is to find out what he's fitted for, what he's most capable of doing—and doing with relish.
—Charles Schwab

The true vocation of a man is to find his way back to himself.
—Hermann Hesse

ABOUT THE AUTHOR

Ford R. Myers is President of Career Potential, LLC. Since 1992, he has been providing professional services in career consulting and executive coaching. After advising thousands of individuals on their careers, Ford drew from his diverse experience to create Career Potential, LLC—a powerful new approach to career management.

Ford has been quoted and featured in the *Wall Street Journal*, the *Chicago Tribune*, the *New York Times*, the *Philadelphia Inquirer*, the *Washington Post, Inc., Fortune, Money, U.S. News & World Report*, and *Crain's Investment News*, among other publications.

Corporate and speaking clients include The Vanguard Group, Sunoco, Radian Group, PJM Interconnection, the Society for Human Resource Management, Career Management Alliance, Association of Career Professionals International, Princeton University, International Society for Performance Improvement, and Harvard University Alumni Association.

Ford has appeared as a career management expert on many television and radio programs, such as NBC-TV, Fox-TV, CBS-TV, Comcast-TV, CBS Radio Network, Clear Channel Radio Network, and Infinity Broadcasting.

His education includes a Bachelor's Degree in Communications, and a Master's Degree in Human Resource Development.

Visit Ford at www.careerpotential.com and www.fordmyers.com.

HOW TO REACH US

Ford R. Myers can help you *Get the Job You Want, Even When No One's Hiring!*

If you would like more information about how Ford and his team at Career Potential, LLC can help you or your organization, please visit www.careerpotential.com. There, you will find full descriptions of the following offerings:

- Corporate Career Development Seminars, which help organizations attract, develop and retain premium talent for lasting marketplace success
- Career Coaching Programs for Individuals, including powerful one, three, and six-month career transition and job search programs
- Career Store, including products and services that help you take charge of your career, create the work you love, and earn what you deserve
- Online Job Search Tools, which help you leverage the best career-related technologies on the web
- Speaking Information, including a full list of presentation topics and booking procedures
- Career GPS Self-Assessment, which helps you quickly map your career goals, plans and strategies
- Career-Building Articles, including a wide range of practical, high-impact career topics
- TV and Radio Interviews, with educational segments on career management and job search strategies
- Media Kit, including useful information for journalists, bloggers, and interviewers

To reach Ford and his team, please send an e-mail to contact@careerpotential.com or call toll-free: 1-888-967-5762.

INDEX